HAWAII

Orchids fill the garden at Durkee's Coffeeland Bed & Breakfast on the Big Island of Hawaii.

FROMMER'S

BED AND BREAKFAST GUIDES

HAWAII

OAHU, MAUI, KAUAI, MOLOKAI, HAWAII

BY LUCY POSHEK

Photographed by Lucy Poshek

DESIGNED AND PRODUCED BY
ROBERT R. REID AND TERRY BERGER

MACMILLAN • USA

Published by Macmillan Travel
A Prentice Hall Macmillan Company
15 Columbus Circle
New York, NY 10023

MACMILLAN is a registered trademark of Macmillan, Inc.

Library of Congress Card No. 94-78857
ISBN 0-02-860064-9

A Robert Reid Associates production
Typeset in Bodoni Book by Monotype Composition Company, Baltimore
Produced by Mandarin Offset, Hong Kong
Printed in Hong Kong

1 2 3 4 5 6 7 8 9 10

CONTENTS

AUTHOR'S NOTE

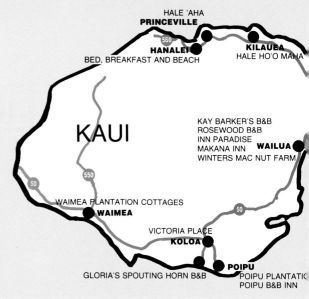

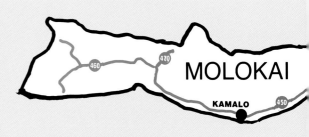

When you first arrive at a Hawaiian-style bed and breakfast, don't be surprised if your host greets you with a hug and a big *aloha* smile. At the door you'll be gently reminded to remove your shoes (an old Oriental custom still practiced widely throughout the islands), leaving them alongside the growing line-up of abandoned sandals and tennies. Padding barefoot into your new home-away-from-home, you'll find your guest room or cottage brightened with colorful tropical flowers cut fresh from the garden. Your host may invite you to go out and pick your own papayas and bananas right off their trees. In the morning, you'll awaken to a symphony of exotic birds and arise to an *aloha* breakfast of Hawaiian coffee (usually Kona or macadamia nut), tropical juices, fresh fruits, and homemade breads.

These are only a few of the differences you'll find between B&B's on the mainland and those in Hawaii. Since the mid-1980s, B&B's have been sprouting up all over Hawaii, creating a more personal and affordable alternative to the big hotels. Whether it's at a homestay, private cottage, or country inn, *informality* is the key word. You won't find a lot of fussy architecture, frilly rooms or long lists of rules on island B&B's. You will, however, find ample amenities, caring hosts, unmatched scenery, and a chance to experience Hawaii in the most intimate way possible. Instead of removing yourself from the local culture as you are at many large resorts, staying at a B&B gives you the chance to get a closer look at the real Hawaii.

Among the hundreds of B&B's now flourishing throughout the islands, there are three basic types: The most common is a homestay, which consists of one to three rooms (often with their own private entrances) in the host's home, with a served continental breakfast included. The second type is an individual cottage adjacent to the host's home (usually called a vacation rental in Hawaii) where breakfast provisions are left in the kitchen for guests to prepare at their leisure. Third and least common are the larger country inns similar to those on the mainland.

Many homestays and cottages are in residential neighborhoods with no identifying signs to set them apart from the other houses. Some are so private that they can only be booked through a reservation service. Their architecture varies from contemporary to suburban to old plantation design. The décor is usually a fresh tropical or country cottage style. Almost all provide a surprisingly wide range of amenities such as televisions, VCR's, telephones, small room refrigerators, afternoon refreshments,

and complimentary beach equipment. Most B&B's are open year round, and many offer discounted rates for weekly stays, so be sure to ask. Some even operate their own reservation services and can even arrange discounted car rentals as well.

When talking to your hosts, you'll hear the following Hawaiian phrases over and over: *Aloha*, of course, is used when greeting someone or saying goodbye. (It can also mean love and compassion.) *Mahalo* means thank you. A *hale* (HAH-lay) is a house. A *lanai* can refer to a porch, veranda, courtyard, or balcony. And when given directions— *makai* (mah-KAI) means toward the sea, whereas *mauka* (MAU-kah) is toward the mountains.

Whether it's due to the balmy climate, the fragrant air, or the slower pace, Hawaiian B&B hosts have an unmatched spirit of *aloha* that is positively infectious. Assuredly, you will remember their warm hospitality long after your vacation is over.

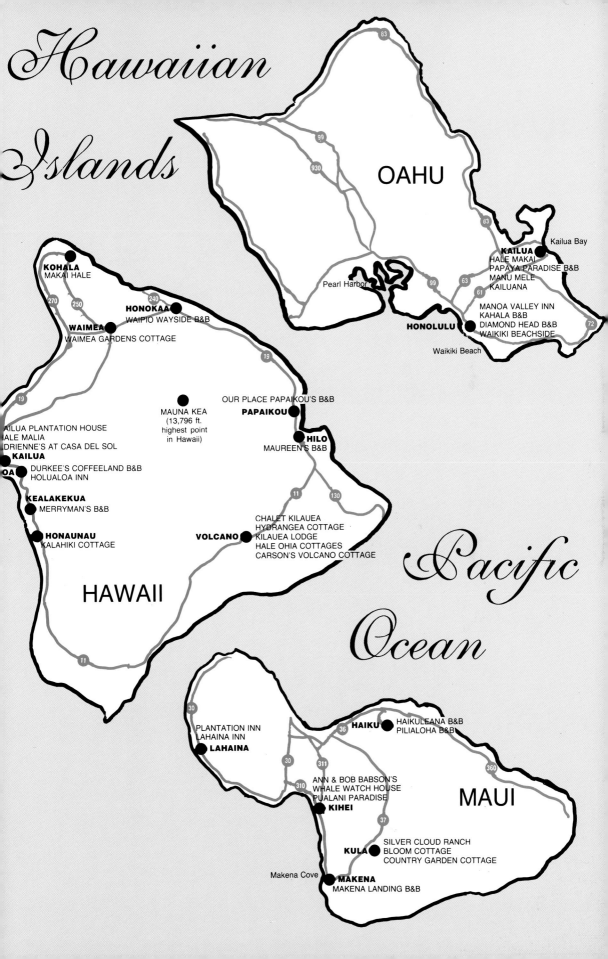

Hawaiian
Islands

Pacific

Ocean

OAHU

83

99

930

83

KAILUA
HALE MAKAI
PAPAYA PARADISE B&B
MANU MELE
KAILUANA

63

61

Kailua Bay

MANOA VALLEY INN
KAHALA B&B
DIAMOND HEAD B&B
WAIKIKI BEACHSIDE

72

Pearl Harbor

99

HONOLULU

Waikiki Beach

KOHALA
MAKAI HALE

270   250

240

HONOKAA
WAIPIO WAYSIDE B&B

WAIMEA
WAIMEA GARDENS COTTAGE

19

MAUNA KEA
(13,796 ft.
highest point
in Hawaii)

OUR PLACE PAPAIKOU'S B&B
PAPAIKOU

HILO
MAUREEN'S B&B

KAILUA PLANTATION HOUSE
HALE MALIA
ADRIENNE'S AT CASA DEL SOL

KAILUA
OA

DURKEE'S COFFEELAND B&B
HOLUALOA INN

KEALAKEKUA
MERRYMAN'S B&B

HONAUNAU
KALAHIKI COTTAGE

11   130

CHALET KILAUEA
HYDRANGEA COTTAGE
KILAUEA LODGE
HALE OHIA COTTAGES
CARSON'S VOLCANO COTTAGE

VOLCANO

HAWAII

11

30

PLANTATION INN
LAHAINA INN

LAHAINA

36

HAIKU

HAIKULEANA B&B
PILIALOHA B&B

30

311

360

ANN & BOB BABSON'S
WHALE WATCH HOUSE
PUALANI PARADISE

310

KIHEI

MAUI

37

SILVER CLOUD RANCH
BLOOM COTTAGE
COUNTRY GARDEN COTTAGE

KULA

Makena Cove

MAKENA
MAKENA LANDING B&B

View of Honolulu from the veranda of Manoa Valley Inn.

OAHU

Oahu, the Gathering Place, is indeed the most populated and visited island in Hawaii. However, because of the overwhelming number of big hotels in Honolulu, you will find relatively few bed and breakfasts here. Waikiki, for instance, has virtually no B&B's, so we have included an intimate boutique hotel for those who wish to stay close to the action in this world-famous district.

There are a small number of delightful B&B's tucked away in various residential neighborhoods of Honolulu and in the quiet bedroom community of Kailua, twenty minutes away. Situated on Windward Oahu—the island's lush, mountainous eastern side—Kailua offers one of the finest beaches and top windsurfing spots on Oahu.

The Craftsman-style mansion.

The second-floor parlor.

MANOA VALLEY INN

A shady veranda overlooks Honolulu

This historic mansion is the best choice on Oahu for those who prefer country inn-style B&B's. Located in the foothills north of Honolulu near the University of Hawaii, it is also convenient to a special part of Honolulu that often gets overlooked—the beautiful Manoa Valley.

Built by an Iowa lumberman in 1915, when Hawaii was still a territory of the United States, the Manoa Valley Inn features large, inviting porches, lava-rock walls and pillars, and decorative wood corbels. The three-story inn is filled with antiques that are blended with modern comforts such as terry robes and electronic closet safes.

Each guest room is named for an individual that was a part of Hawaii's early history. The Guild Suite is the largest and has a Victorian-style sitting area in addition to its many-windowed bedroom. The Cooke, Baldwin and Moore rooms, with their distinc-

Left, the antique bed in the exotic Cook Room.

tive period beds, are also popular. The third-floor rooms, once the servants quarters, are smaller and share a bath.

Downstairs you will find a living room with a lava rock fireplace, a TV parlor, and a billiards room. There is also a separate guest cottage that is all but hidden off the veranda. Complimentary sherry is found in a red velvet-furnished parlor on the second floor.

But the biggest attraction at the inn is its large, shady veranda—or lanai as it is called in Hawaii—where guests can enjoy their continental breakfast or gather for afternoon wine and cheese. Scattered with wicker chairs, a porch swing, and potted orchids, the peaceful lanai is where most guests gravitate to watch the sun set on Diamond Head and the city skyline.

MANOA VALLEY INN, 2001 Vancouver Drive, Honolulu, HI 96822; (800) 634-5115; (808) 947-6019; Lisa Hookano-Holly, general manager; Leina'ala ("Lei") Kim, innkeeper. Seven rooms, including three with shared bath, and one cottage with private bath. Rates: $110 to $190, including continental breakfast and afternoon wine and cheese. Children under 12 not recommended; no pets; smoking allowed on veranda only; Japanese spoken; all credit cards accepted. University of Hawaii, Manoa Valley Theater, Paradise Park, Lyon Arboretum, and the hike to Manoa Falls nearby. Keo's Thai Cuisine, Waioli Tea Room, and Cafe Brio recommended for dining.

DIRECTIONS: from H-1 east, exit at University Ave. (24B) and turn left. After the second stoplight, turn left on Vancouver Dr.

KAHALA BED & BREAKFAST

Bordering Waialae Golf Course

The Kahala district, on the far side of Diamond Head from Waikiki, boasts some of the most exclusive homes on the island. One drive down lovely, tree-lined Kahala Avenue will make it clear why such celebrities as Tom Selleck have chosen to live here.

In the heart of this district, overlooking the Waialae Golf Course, is the Kahala Bed & Breakfast. The elegant gray and white home is built around an impeccably-landscaped courtyard with a long, sparkling lap pool. Arching over the pool is a footbridge that leads you to your private, luxurious guest wing.

Both of the spacious suites are formally appointed in a refined East-West style. The huge downstairs living room is a sea of soft green carpeting complemented by cream-colored sofas and moss-patterned chairs. A tall vase of fresh flowers reflects off the glass dining room table while Buddha sculptures and carved Oriental cabinets add a touch of the East. A wall of French doors opens to a lanai that faces the golf course across the canal.

The house fronts on the Waialae Golf Course.

The living room of the upstairs suite is also a showcase, with crisp blue and white as the prevailing theme. Like the downstairs suite, there is an indulgent amount of room to spread out here, with an extra bedroom to spare.

The hosts, Mary and Joe, are fourth and fifth generation *kamaainas*, or long-time residents of Hawaii. After their initial welcome, they leave their guests with total privacy and a generous number of amenities—a television and VCR, a fully equipped kitchen with breakfast fixings in the refrigerator, large dressing areas, and even wall safes.

For entertainment, Mary and Joe will direct you to the luxurious Kahala Hilton, one block away, where there are numerous fine restaurants, a public beach, and several-times-a-day dolphin shows.

Left, above, the living room of the Upstairs Suite. Below, the living room of the Downstairs Suite.

KAHALA BED & BREAKFAST, Honolulu, Oahu; *represented by Hawaii's Best Bed & Breakfasts*; (800) 262-9912; (808) 885-4550; two suites (one with two bedrooms), each with private bath and full kitchen. Rates: $100, double, including self-serve continental breakfast (2-night minimum). No children; no pets; smoking allowed outside only; no credit cards. 18-hole golf course at Waialae Country Club. The Kahala Mall, Kahala Hilton, and Waialae Beach within walking distance.

DIRECTIONS: sent prior to departure.

The house is built around a courtyard and pool.

The Girls' Room, with a koa bed that once belonged to Princess Ruth.

DIAMOND HEAD B&B

Lots of family heirlooms

This sprawling older home is nestled in the foothills of Diamond Head within sight of Waikiki. It is the kind of Hawaiian home that was typical fifty years ago—airy rooms and polished wood floors flowing out to a wide lanai; and in the yard, a profusion of huge tropical trees spreading their web of sweetly scented shade over the sloping lawn.

Joanne, the hostess, has collected many interesting family heirlooms during her 40-odd years in Hawaii. Displayed in glass cases in the dining room are countless old bottles accumulated during her husband's days as a plantation manager. One bedroom contains a larger-than-king-size, four-poster koa bed that once belonged to Princess Ruth, a member of Hawaiian royalty (and woman of wide girth). Most of the paintings on the walls were done by Joanne, an artist and active supporter of the arts in Honolulu.

Left, the relaxing back yard.

Both of the upstairs guest rooms are spacious and unassuming, with Hawaiian-style wooden doors sliding open to private lanais. The "Girls' Room" faces the dark green cliffs of Diamond Head while the "Boys' Room" has a view of Waikiki through the branches of an ancient plumeria tree. Televisions and refrigerators are hidden in the closets.

Also on hand to greet guests is Sumiko, Joanne's longtime family housekeeper. Together they prepare a variety of breakfasts, and sometimes guests are treated to salmon caught by Joanne and Sumiko on their twice-a-year fishing trips to the Rogue River.

If you like to walk, this is about the only B&B on the island where a car would not be that necessary. Kapiolani Park, the beach, and access to "The Bus" line (which goes around the island) are just down the hill.

DIAMOND HEAD B&B, Honolulu, Oahu; *represented by Hawaii's Best Bed & Breakfasts;* (800) 262-9912; (808) 885-4550. Two rooms, each with private bath. Rates: $80, single; $95, double, including breakfast (one-night stay $20 extra). Children over 8 welcome. Smoking allowed outside on lanai only; Japanese spoken; no credit cards. Kapiolani Park, Diamond Head Crater, Kaimana Beach, Honolulu Zoo, Waikiki Aquarium, and "The Bus" line are all within walking distance. New Otani Kaimana Beach Hotel and Hale Vietnam recommended for dining.

DIRECTIONS: sent prior to departure.

Overleaf, a view of Waikiki from the Boys' Room lanai.

A guest room.

A Chinese secretary in the lounge.

WAIKIKI BEACHSIDE

A small, intimate hotel on the beach

Although not a bed and breakfast in the traditional sense, this is one of the smallest and most personal hotels you will find in Waikiki. Elegant and intimate, the Waikiki Beachside provides a soothing oasis for visitors who want to experience, but not be overwhelmed by, the action on Waikiki Beach.

This boutique hotel is so unobtrusive from Kalakaua Avenue that one could easily pass it by unnoticed. But upon entering the columned marble foyer with its luxurious Chinese carpets and chandeliers, it's immediately obvious that this is not any ordinary Waikiki hotel.

The Chinoiserie décor—a combination of East and West styles—is highlighted by beautiful Tai Ping carpets and exquisite antique furnishings, all personally selected by owners Jane and André Tatibouet (also the owners of Aston Hotels). In the lobby, for instance, is a nineteenth-century French sculpture and antique Chinese altar table. Bronze

Left, the opulent entrance hall.

lions flank the stairs that lead up to a serene lounge and an adjoining courtyard. Here you will find exquisitely-carved Oriental screens and a wonderful Chinese desk which guests are free to use.

Also Oriental in flavor, the guest rooms are small but tastefully cast in soft peach tones with black trim. Televisions, VCR's and refrigerators are hidden inside an armoire. The bathrooms are particularly plush, with sleek showers, hidden safes, second phones, and fine soaps. Kimono robes are provided, and a tropical shell is left on your pillow at night.

The ocean-view rooms are clearly more rewarding than the non-view rooms. From your balcony you will have an unobstructed view of the best stretch of Waikiki Beach (across the street) and all its activity—surfers, outrigger canoes, catamarans, tourists, and a surprisingly pretty beach.

WAIKIKI BEACHSIDE, 2452 Kalakaua Avenue, Honolulu, Oahu, HI 96815; (800) 922-7866; (808) 931-2100; Donna Wheeler, general manager. Seventy-nine rooms, all with private baths, air conditioning, and refrigerator. Rates: $160 to $290, max. 2 persons, including coffee and Danish. Children not encouraged; smoking allowed, but non-smoking rooms can be requested; all credit cards accepted. Concierge, voice mail, twice daily maid service.   All the attractions of Waikiki Beach at hand. Hyatt Regency allows charging privileges for dining..

DIRECTIONS: from H-1, exit at Nimitz Hwy. which becomes Ala Moana. Proceed through Waikiki to Kalakaua Ave. and turn right. Look for the hotel on the left after Ulunui St. Park in front to check in.

Overleaf, looking down on Waikiki Beach from the balcony of a guest room.

HALE MAKAI

The true spirit of *aloha*

If you wish to experience a true homestay-style B&B, Hale Makai (pronounced HAH-lay mah-KAI) is an excellent place to begin. With their warm spirit of *aloha*, hosts Ron and Donna make one of the nicest welcoming committees on the island. Ron, an interior designer, and Donna, retired from 29 years as a violinist with the Honolulu Symphony, have lived in Kailua for 25 years, so they know the area well.

Left, a Hawaiian sunset as it looks from Hale Makai.

Hosts Ron and Donna on the front lanai.

A guest room.

Their comfortable, unpretentious home is in a quiet residential area less than a block from Kailua Beach. Two homey bedrooms are set up for only one couple or group at a time. Two shady lanais and a living room filled to the brim with interesting books, paintings, and musical instruments offer additional room to spread out or visit with Ron and Donna. As there is no television in their peaceful home, conversation takes precedence here—an almost forgotten, back-to-the-basics B&B feature.

Ron and Donna encourage their guests to rise early at least one morning to experience a Kailua Bay sunrise. The sweeping uncrowded, crescent-shaped bay has been rated by *Condé Nast Traveler* as one of the nation's top ten beaches. So, even if you're not a morning person, sunrises here are a must. You can stroll through the fine, soft sand, witness the dramatically changing sky, and return just in time for an *aloha* breakfast served by Ron out on the plant-filled lanai. Don't be surprised if Donna takes your snapshot and sends it to you later with a thank-you note—a thoughtful memento of your morning on Kailua Bay.

HALE MAKAI, Kailua, Oahu; *represented by Hawaii's Best Bed & Breakfasts*, (800) 262-9912; (808) 885-4550. Two rooms with one shared bath for up to 4 persons (when traveling together). Rates: $65, double, including continental *aloha* breakfast (2-night minimum). Children over 15 welcome; no pets; no smoking in house; no credit cards. Walk to swimming beach; tennis and golf nearby. Buzz's and Assaggio's recommended for dining.

DIRECTIONS: sent prior to departure.

Papaya, the food of the gods.

PAPAYA PARADISE BED & BREAKFAST

Hearty breakfasts and leisurely days

Until a blight wiped out the flourishing papaya trees in Bob and Jeanette Martz's yard five years ago, this B&B was well-known for its abundance of papayas. The hosts made so many culinary uses out of the sublime fruit that Jeanette was referred to as the "papaya lady." But, says Jeanette, "Even though the papayas are gone, people keep coming back."

Their suburban home is about a half-mile from Kailua Bay. Guests pass through a side wing of the house (where Precious, the resident cat, usually greets them with a yawn) to reach a large courtyard where two smallish guest rooms have their own entrances.

With a view of the swimming pool, spa, land-scaped yard (now re-planted with new papaya saplings), and lush Mount Olomana beyond, the shady courtyard is where guests spend their leisure time reading or enjoying Bob's hearty breakfasts. Bob, a retired naval officer, whips up soldier-sized breakfasts of pancakes, eggs and home-fries, or perhaps his "SOS" specialty—ground beef and gravy over toast.

Guests here have been known to stay for extended periods—sometimes up to a month at a time. They come precisely because there is *not* a lot of action going on here. A little swim in the bay, a cup of Hawaiian coffee at the old-fashioned neighborhood market . . . and it's time to return to Papaya Paradise with a good paperback.

PAPAYA PARADISE BED & BREAKFAST, 395 Auwinala Road, Kailua, Oahu, HI 96734; (808) 261-0316; Bob and Jeanette Martz, hosts. Two rooms, both with private entrances and baths, TV, air conditioning, and ceiling fans. Rates: $65 to $70, including full breakfast. Three-night minimum. Children over age 6 permitted; no pets; smoking permitted outdoors only; cash or traveler's checks only. Water sports, tennis and golf nearby. Buzz's and Harry's Cafe recommended for dining.

DIRECTIONS: from Honolulu, take Route 61 through the Pali Tunnel into Kailua. Turn right on Kailua Rd. until it becomes Wanaao Rd. and then meets Kakahiaka St. Turn right, then right again on Auwinala Rd.

Guest wing and pool.

The pool and one of two guest rooms with private entrances.

Yellow Hibiscus, the state flower.

MANU MELE

One block to the beach

Not only do a variety of tropical birds flutter about the feeder at Manu Mele, but one very friendly little fellow—Manu the Myna Bird—has been known to greet guests right in their rooms. It's no wonder that *manu mele*, the Hawaiian name for this B&B home, translates into "bird song."

Located on Windward Oahu, Manu Mele is on a somewhat busy thoroughfare at the far end of Kailua Bay. The L-shaped house faces a courtyard and swimming pool which is nicely lit at night. Two sparkling clean guest rooms have their own private entries off the courtyard. A nearby footpath makes a one-block beeline to the beach.

Hostess Carol Isaacs has lived in Hawaii since the 1960s but still has traces of a British accent from growing up in England. Friendly and easygoing, she is helpful at directing you to all the best spots, yet leaves you with a balance of privacy. Guests do not gather for breakfast in the morning; rather, a self-serve breakfast is left in the bar refrigerator of each room. Both units also have microwaves, coffee makers, and televisions.

The yard is filled with Tahitian gardenias, night-blooming jasmine, and yellow hibiscus, which is Hawaii's state flower. In addition to the myna birds are Java sparrows, cardinals, rice birds, doves, and bulbuls. Guests awaken to exotic coos, chirps and, naturally, plenty of *manu mele*.

MANU MELE, 153 Kailuana Place, Kailua, Oahu, HI 96734; (808) 262-0016; Carol and Charles Isaacs, owners. Two rooms, each with private bath. Rates: $55 to $65, including continental breakfast for the first 3 days. No children; no pets (a friendly Irish setter is in residence); smoking permitted; no credit cards. Hiking, golfing, and water sports at Kailua Bay nearby. Assagio's, Saeng's, and Jaron's recommended for dining.

DIRECTIONS: from Honolulu, take Route 61 through the Pali Tunnel and Kailua until it ends at S. Kalaheo Ave. Turn left and continue 1.5 miles to Kailuana Pl., on the right.

Breakfast-sitting room.

KAILUANA

One of Oahu's rare beachfront B&Bs

If many of the private homes on Oahu look rather unremarkable from the street, it's because their prettiest features are hidden behind their gates. Kailuana is a classic example: Your first sight upon entering is a long, graceful swimming pool with an inviting spa at one end and a solitary Greek bust at the other. The effect is striking.

Inside, the sophisticated home is a study in neutral colors—creams, taupes, ivory, and earth-toned collectibles gathered from around the world. A wall of windows faces a wide front l vn and Kailua Bay beyond. Kailuana, by the wa   is one of the only beachfront B&B's on Oahu.

Guests are free to use the formal family living room or the library with its interesting array of Hawaiiana books, but they usually feel most comfortable in the more casual, ocean-view living room where breakfast is served.   Joanne, the hostess, once owned an antique shop and still likes to use a variety of antique linens at her breakfast table. Also on display nearby is her old-fashioned doll house which is exquisitely detailed.

Two well-tended guest rooms, tastefully furnished in wicker and rattan, are on opposite wings of the house from the hosts' private quarters. Sliding glass doors open from the bedrooms out to the poolside, and the bathroom has its own entrance directly from the beach. In each room is a welcome plate of baked goodies and fruit.

In addition to the swimming pool and spa, a dry sauna is also available. But guests frequently opt for the soft sand beach right outside their door. Referring to the legendary sunrises on Kailua Bay, Joanne says, "I was going to call this house 'Pink Sunrise,' but the Hawaiian translation is about six sentences long!"

Left, view of Kailua Bay from the terrace.

The classically elegant pool.

KAILUANA, Kailua, Oahu; *represented by Hawaii's Best Bed & Breakfasts;* (800) 262-9912; (808) 885-4550. Two rooms with one shared bath for up to 4 adults (when traveling together). Rates: $125, double, including breakfast (2-night minimum). Children; no pets; no smoking; Bulgarian and Russian spoken; no credit cards. All water sports, including windsurfing, nearby. Harry's Cafe and Buzz's recommended for dining.

DIRECTIONS: sent prior to departure.

Makena Cove, home to Makena Landing B&B (pages 36–37).

MAUI

Maui's bed and breakfast accommodations can be roughly divided into
two geographic areas: The coastal
stretch from Makena to Lahaina,
and the rural, upcountry communities on the slopes of Haleakala, a
ten thousand-foot dormant volcano.
While the coast offers sugar-white
beaches where the swimming and
sunning can't be beat, it is also
somewhat busy and overdeveloped.
Though upcountry Maui doesn't
have the beaches, its rolling hills
and green pastures make a peaceful
retreat from the tourist scene.

Though they appear fairly close
to each other, it can take anywhere
from forty minutes to an hour to get
from upcountry Maui to the
beaches. And the colorful old
whaling town of Lahaina is a good
forty minutes from Kihei. It's a
good idea to spend some time in
each area, as they are worlds apart
in atmosphere.

ANN & BOB BABSON'S

A Jacuzzi with a view

Ann and Bob Babson really bend over backwards to help their guests become acquainted with Maui. Having moved here from Marin County only a few years ago, these friendly hosts still have a fresh enthusiasm for the island and are glad to share all their local knowledge with you.

Located just a mile uphill from the ocean in Maui Meadows, their modern wood home is comfortable and informal, landscaped with a profusion of papaya trees and bougainvillea. Two bedrooms—The Bougainvillea Suite and Molokini Master Suite—are on the second level of the main house, where there is also a common living room, dining-breakfast area, and ocean-view, whale-watching lanai. For those who prefer less socializing, two non-B&B rental units—The Hibiscus Hideaway Apartment (with its own entry downstairs) and Sunset Cottage (adjacent to the main house)—are also available.

Among the variety of accommodations, the Molokini Master Suite is the most unique. Like the living room, this bedroom is hexagonally-shaped and lined with a wall of windows. From the bed, which is spotlighted by an overhead skylight, you have a panoramic ocean view. Even from the huge Jacuzzi tub in the bathroom there is a view of Molokini, a tiny island off the coast of Maui.

Upon arrival, Bob and Ann greet their guests with a welcome glass of passion-orange-guava juice. Bob provides a wealth of introductory information that they have personally compiled—driving tours, fact sheets, best beaches (including a clothing-optional hideaway), and local restaurant tips. They offer everything from free laundry service to assistance in making reservations elsewhere throughout the islands—a part of their statewide reservation service.

Left, main house with papaya trees in fruit.

View of the ocean from the lanai, overlooking Maui Meadows.

Molokini Master Suite with skylight and deck.

ANN & BOB BABSON'S VACATION RENTALS, 3371 Keha Drive, Kihei, Maui, HI 96753; (800) 824-6409; (808) 874-1166; Fax (808) 879-7906; Ann and Bob Babson, hosts. Two suites, one-bedroom apartment, all with private baths and one two-bedroom cottage, with 2 baths. Rates: $65 to $95, including breakfast (in B&B units). Three-night minimum. Children allowed in cottage only; no pets (one indoor cat in residence); no smoking; no credit cards. White sand beaches, snorkeling lagoons, hiking, golf, and tennis nearby. List of restaurants sent with confirmation.

DIRECTIONS: from Kahului Airport, follow signs to Kihei. Head south on Hwy. 31 (Piilani Hwy.) for exactly 6 miles from Hwy. 350. Turn left at Mapu Pl., left at Kupulau Dr., then right on Keha Dr. B&B is on the left.

WHALE WATCH HOUSE

A tropical fantasy come true

Maui locals always speak fondly of the Whale Watch House, and for good reason: Its *hale*, or thatched hut, is the most classic, Polynesian-style accommodation you will find anywhere on Maui. This romantic haven is a tropical fantasy come true.

Hidden away in the unlikely suburb of Maui Meadows, the *hale* is one of four theme-inspired units featured at the Whale Watch House. The other three—in more subdued tropical, Oriental and American themes, with their own private entrances and decks—are in the main house. The property, owned by spirited hosts Patrick and Patricia, is verdant, to say the least. Multi-colored bougainvillea frames the parking area. Huge bamboo shoots, papaya trees, ginger, and hibiscus practically envelope the gravel path that leads to the *hale*.

Built before a natural lagoon-like swimming pool and gazebo (the site of many weddings), the *hale* has a steep thatched roof which is beautifully abloom with creeping trumpet vines. It has a wooden lanai that almost extends over the pool. The rustic, woven lauhala interior is straight out of a Hawaiian romance novel. Hovering among the sloping rafters, overlooking the living room and kitchen, is an open loft bedroom with gauzy mosquito netting poised over the bed.

Patricia, an artist, originally used the *hale* as a studio in which to paint. Since transforming it into a B&B, she has artfully decorated the *hale* and lush grounds with whimsical little details—a knight on horseback with his lady perched atop the gazebo

Hale's Polynesian-style living room.

roof; a guardian angel topiary tucked into a stray pathway; an armoire with a trompe l'oeil painting inside. On the ocean-view lanai of her home, where breakfast is served, a life-size butler stands unnervingly at the entry. If Pat is out, arriving guests will find the butler holding a welcome note on his tray.

WHALE WATCH HOUSE, Kihei, Maui; *represented by Hawaii's Best Bed & Breakfasts;* (800) 262-9912; (808) 885-4550. One *hale* (thatched cottage), a one-bedroom studio, and two bedrooms, all with private baths and entrances. Rates: $65 to $85, including continental breakfast on weekdays (2-night minimum). No children; no pets (two cats on premises); no smoking; no credit cards. Five-minute drive to Wailea beaches.

DIRECTIONS: sent prior to departure.

Left, Hale's idyllic lanai and pool in classic Polynesian style.

View of Kahoolawe from breakfast lanai.

Life-sized butler at entry of main house.

A Balinese "Protector of the House."

PUALANI PARADISE ISLAND COTTAGE

Hawaiian décor with Balinese accents

Located in the suburban neighborhood of Maui Meadows, this single, one-bedroom cottage sits adjacent to the residence of young hosts Charles and Merrily Webb, a busy young working couple.

Merrily, who spent a lot of time in Indonesia, has added some intriguing Balinese accents to the Hawaiian décor. Suspended from the bedroom ceiling is an exotic doll that serves as "protector of the home." Vases of fresh halyconia add splashes of color here and there, while skylights bring in the sun.

The contemporary cottage is typical of the other homes in Maui Meadows—architecturally unremarkable, but comfortably designed to provide all away-from-home essentials. A small living room is supplied with television, VCR, videos, stereo, games, books, and telephone. Adjoining this is a full kitchen with refrigerator and microwave. Guests also have access to a washer and dryer.

One of the two cottage entrances opens out to a swimming pool area which guests are invited to use. Actually, it is Keala, the family's golden retriever, who uses the pool most often. Whether it's to show off his swan dive or belly flop, Keala will find any excuse to leap into the pool and go for a dog paddle. Many guests and their kids spend the entire afternoon just playing with Keala.

As for other water sports, Merrily will happily steer you to a wealth of ocean activities at the beach, only a few miles down the hill.

Front door decorations.

Left, above, Keala, the diving dog, loves the pool. Below, a charmingly decorated guest room.

PUALANI PARADISE ISLAND COTTAGE, 3134 Hoomua Drive, Kihei, HI 96753; (808) 875-8522; Merrily and Charles Webb, owners. One-bedroom cottage with kitchen and private bath. Rate: $75, including self-serve continental breakfast; $10 for third person. Three-night minimum. Children welcome; smoking allowed outside only; no credit cards. All water sports, shopping, bicycling and whale watching nearby.

DIRECTIONS: in Maui Meadows area above Wailea. Directions sent upon confirmation.

A beach front home now hosting bed and breakfast guests.
(See also pages 28–29.)

MAKENA LANDING B&B

Maui's only oceanfront B&B

Makena Landing is the only oceanfront bed and breakfast in Maui, and what a spot it is. Built right next to Makena Landing, beyond Wailea, the protected cove here offers terrific snorkeling and even several underwater caves. Although the tiny island of Molokini—another popular snorkeling spot—looks invitingly close, many commercial scuba boats choose to anchor directly in front of the B&B. Within walking distance is a sandy cove, and only a short drive away are some of Maui's most beautiful and uncrowded beaches, including the much-photographed Big Beach.

Owned by Boogie and Vi Lu'uwai, this property is also unique because it has been in Boogie's family for seven generations, dating back to the early 1800s. Vi and Boogie spent years coming to Makena

Left, above, the front yard overlooks a coastline of volcanic rocks. Below, a knotty cedar guest room with an inviting deck.

Landing for their family vacations (their neighbors are still their own family members), and then wound up settling here when they retired. Their cedar home was redesigned to accommodate B&B guests, so now the two casual upstairs bedrooms have their own private entrances from an outside stairway. But guests have free use of the whole downstairs area as well, including the kitchen and covered lanai with its long picnic table. You are treated like one of the family and can even take Punani, the resident golden retriever, for a walk.

The whole setting is loose and relaxing, with the ocean providing a peaceful focus. Vi says, "We have a lot of *mana* here—the power of the environment. If you let yourself go, you'll feel it."

February to April is the whale watching season, and many guests book up to a year in advance. You couldn't get better seats for the show than this.

MAKENA LANDING B&B, 5100 Makena Road, Makena, Maui, HI 96753; (808) 879-6286; Boogie and Vi Lu'uwai, owners. Two rooms with shared balcony, private baths and private entrances. Rates: $70 (plus 10% tax), including full breakfast and snacks. Three-night minimum. Children 12 and over allowed; no smoking; no pets (one Golden Retriever in residence); Hawaiian spoken; no credit cards. All water sports just steps away. (Bring your own snorkel equipment or rent from Snorkel Bob's nearby.) Golf courses nearby. Sea Watch and The Prince recommended for dining.

DIRECTIONS: map and directions sent with confirmation.

Beautiful guest room no. 15.

Al fresco dining on the lanai.

THE PLANTATION INN

New Orleans ambience

The Plantation Inn is one of those rare finds in Hawaii—an impeccably run inn that combines the luxuries of a fine hotel with the friendly, caring intimacy of a B&B. What a refreshing sight!

Reminiscent more of New Orleans than Hawaii, the cheerful, plantation-style inn is built around an attractive central courtyard, pavilion lounge, swimming pool, and spa. The newer of the two buildings is set back from the street, providing maximum peace and quiet. Painted light grey with white trim, both buildings feature second-story verandas that are filled prettily with greenery and white wicker furnishings.

Whereas the exterior is quite the Southern belle, the guest rooms vary widely in their themes. Ranging from Victorian to Oriental to European, each room and suite is beautifully appointed down to its spotless tiled bathroom. Room Fifteen, for example, is a study in French-Chinese elegance, with a king-sized canopied bed, a whimsical, Napoleonic love seat, an old-fashioned Oriental writing desk, and

Left, the elaborately beautiful pool beckons all.

striking arrangement of oversized, sculptured fruit on the glass coffee table. Many rooms have stained glass framing the French doors that open to their private balconies. Every room has a small refrigerator with complimentary refreshments hidden inside.

The inn also boasts one of the top-rated restaurants on Maui—Gerard's—and guests can enjoy discounts on dinners here. Set on the streetside veranda, Gerard's offers a romantic setting and fabulous French cuisine. This is also where guests return for their complimentary buffet breakfast.

Afternoon coffee awaits in the shady, tiled pavilion, which is festooned by a carousel horse. After shopping on Lahaina's bustling Front Street, less than two blocks away, the inn offers a peaceful respite from the tourist crowds.

THE PLANTATION INN, 174 Lahainaluna Road, Lahaina, Maui, HI 96761; (800) 433-6815; (808) 667-9225; Fax (808) 667-9293; Charles Robinson, manager. Nineteen rooms and suites, all with private baths. Rates: $99 to $179, including extended continental breakfast and discounts at Gerard's Restaurant. Honeymoon and dive packages available. Children welcome; no pets; smoking encouraged on the balconies; French and Spanish spoken; Visa/MasterCard/American Express. All ocean activities, shopping, and historic sites within walking distance. Gerard's Restaurant recommended for dining.

DIRECTIONS: from Kahului Airport, follow signs to Lahaina. Turn left on Lahainaluna Rd. from Hwy. 30. Entrance to inn is on the left (though parking is on Panaewa St.)

Guest room no. 8.

LAHAINA INN

An extraordinary restoration

The Lahaina Inn is a step back to the very civilized world of the 1890s. Situated just down the block from the Plantation Inn, this sumptuous, twelve-room establishment is of the same high caliber—professionally-run, luxurious, and exquisitely-decorated, but is Victorian to the core.

The two-story structure was painstakingly restored by Rick Ralston, who is well-known throughout the islands as both the owner of Crazy Shirts, Inc. and as an avid preservationist. Ralston has restored seven historic mansions in Honolulu, including the former John Guild Inn (now the Manoa Valley Inn). Most of the antiques found throughout the Lahaina Inn are from Ralston's extensive personal collection.

While the reception area occupies the main level, the guest quarters are all found on the second level. Each room has been authentically detailed in turn-of-the-century style, with Oriental rugs atop polished wood floors, romantic period beds of brass or wood, floral wall coverings, lace runners, exquisite bed

Left, the front of the inn faces on Lahainaluna Road.

spreads, antique armoires, and stained-glass lamps. Taped classical music adds the final note of polished refinement. The only departure from the Victorian theme are complimentary *yakutas* (Oriental robes) hanging in the white-tiled bathrooms.

All the guest rooms have balconies with views of either the harbor—a half block away—or the mountains. The harbor-facing balconies, which are more spacious, also overlook the bustling heart of Lahaina, which can be noisy at night but fun in the morning. Everyone avails themselves of an aloha breakfast from the hall sideboard and returns with their trays to survey the scene from balcony rocking chairs.

Adjoining the inn is David Paul's Lahaina Grill, a hot local restaurant which features a creative menu of New American cuisine. Be sure to visit the antique store next door, which is also owned by Rick Ralston.

LAHAINA INN (formerly Lahaina Hotel), 129 Lahainaluna Road, Lahaina, Maui, HI 96761; (800) 669-3444; (808) 661-0577; Fax (808) 667-9480; Kenneth Eisley, general manager. Twelve rooms and suites, all with private baths. Rates: $89 to $129, including continental breakfast. Wedding and honeymoon packages available. Children over 15 accepted; no pets; smoking allowed on lanai only; all credit cards accepted. All ocean activities, beaches, galleries, and restaurants of Lahaina within walking distance. David Paul's Lahaina Grill recommended for dining.

DIRECTIONS: from Kahului Airport, follow Hwy. 31 to Lahaina. Turn left at Lahainaluna Rd. and look for inn on the right.

Overleaf, the stunningly decorated Mauka Room.

SILVER CLOUD RANCH

Ranch-style sit-down breakfasts

Silver Cloud Ranch is about as far removed as you can get from the crowded coastal shoreline of Maui. Situated at the end of a remote, one-lane road off the Kula Highway, this country inn enjoys spectacular vistas from the sweeping slopes of Haleakala across the entire western half of the island. When the clouds roll up and obscure the view, as they often do, the immediate landscape bears an uncanny resemblance to the moors of Scotland.

The nine-acre compound was originally part of the Thompson Ranch, established in 1902. Several of the plantation-style structures have been restored and now provide a wide selection of accommodations. Six bedrooms are in the Plantation Home, which features an elegantly-appointed common room with French doors opening to a long veranda and unhindered view. A short distance away are five more units in the Paniolo Bunkhouse. For those desiring more privacy, there's also the Lanai Cottage adjacent to the main house. This homey cottage features a kitchen, wood-burning stove, ocean-view lanai, and a fire engine-red clawfoot tub. Hosts Sara and Mike Gerry live in a separate bunkhouse on the grounds.

While no longer a working cattle ranch, Silver Cloud still hosts a wide variety of farm animals, including cows, hens, cats, and a pot-bellied pig named Rupert. Sara also keeps a bizarrely sized array of horses: a miniature horse, Shetland pony, and Belgian draft horse.

Guests gather for a full, sit-down breakfast in the garden sunroom of the Plantation Home. Pancakes, Hawaiian sweet bread French toast, or a hearty "paniolo (cowboy) breakfast"—Portuguese sausages, white rice, eggs, fresh fruit, and muffins— are part of the standard fare.

SILVER CLOUD RANCH, RR2 Box 201, Old Thompson Road, Kula, Maui, HI 96790; (808) 878-6101; Fax (808) 878-2132; Mike and Sara Gerry, owners. Eleven rooms and suites, plus a one-bedroom cottage; some with kitchens and fireplaces; all with private baths. Rates: $75 to $135, including full breakfast; $15 for third person. Weddings can be arranged. Children welcome; smoking permitted outside only; no credit cards. Horseback riding available at neighboring ranch. Haleakala Crater and Tedeschi Winery nearby. Kula Lodge, Haliimaile General Store, and Makawao Steak House recommended for dining.

DIRECTIONS: from Kahului Airport, follow Hwy. 37 (Kula Hwy.) past the 16-mile marker to Keokea. Turn left at Grandma's Coffee House, and then immediately fork right on Thompson Rd. Ranch is 1.2 miles on the left.

Bird of Paradise blooms surround the ranch sign.

Dickey, the miniature horse.

Left, the Paniolo Bunkhouse has five guest units. (Paniolo means "Cowboy".)

One of the two guest rooms.

The English country-style living room.

BLOOM COTTAGE

English country style

Bloom Cottage is a romantic gem on the pastoral slopes of Haleakala. Though it was named for the herb and flower garden it sits in, the lovingly-decorated interior is equally springlike.

The quaint cottage sits at three thousand feet on a hill above the home of hosts Herb and Lynne Horner, a friendly *kamaaina* couple. Lynne (who works as an editor of the *Maui News*) intentionally avoided the usual tropical décor and decorated her cottage in a refreshing English country style. "I figure people get enough Hawaiian décor at the hotels," she says. Whitewashed walls, white beamed ceilings, and cedar floors give the cottage a sunny glow. Crisp blue and white-striped cushions on rustic Mexican furnishings, floral curtains, and vases of protea (a locally-grown flower) add to the lovely visual effect.

Everything here is tuned to romance: The fireplace is stocked with wood for those cool upcountry evenings. From the breakfast table you have a *Left, Bloom Cottage and Itty the cat.*

dreamy view of Maalaea Bay, Kahului Bay, and the West Maui Mountains. The television and VCR are equipped with a collection of romantic videos. Heart-shaped collectibles hang on the kitchen wall.

The smaller of the two bedrooms looks like it sprang from *A Child's Garden of Verses*, with old-fashioned children's books on display. The main bedroom is also whitewashed, with a white down quilt and linen pillows atop the four-poster bamboo bed. Tucked into the beams are still more intriguing books. ("I'm just a book freak," admits Lynn.)

A guest of Bloom Cottage once commented, "I've seen twenty things I've never seen in a hotel room." Flannel sheets, interesting magazines, baskets of toiletries, and a sewing basket are only a few of the personal extras provided. You'll even find warm jackets in the closet for the nippy sunrise trip to Haleakala Crater.

BLOOM COTTAGE, 229 Kula Highway, Kula, Maui, HI 96790; (808) 878-1425; Herb and Lynne Horner, owners. Two-bedroom cottage with full kitchen and private bath. Rate: $95, including self-serve continental breakfast. Children over 10 welcome; no pets (two cats on the premises); no smoking; no credit cards. Downhill biking, horseback riding, hiking, Tedeschi Winery, and Haleakala Crater nearby. Restaurants in nearby towns of Makawao and Haliimaile.

DIRECTIONS: from Kahului Airport, follow Hwy. 37 toward Keokea. Between the 15 and 16-mile markers, turn left on Maukanani Rd. and park next to white fence on left corner of road. Cottage is behind hosts' house, and both are white with green trim.

Each of the four guest rooms has a different color scheme.

HAIKULEANA B&B PLANTATION STYLE

A finely restored plantation house

Haikuleana is one of the few historic plantation-style bed and breakfasts found on the islands. Built in 1870 for a plantation doctor, the white house features a classic lanai and red tin roof that contrasts colorfully with the blue sky and surrounding greenery. It has been beautifully restored by Fred Fox, who is also by coincidence a doctor, though now retired. An extremely nice host, Fred always takes time to explain the history of the house to his new guests. Having previously owned a B&B in the Adirondacks, he's already attuned to the fine art of innkeeping.

The graceful interior was tastefully decorated by the inn's manager and interior designer, Allyn Gardner. The foyer, living room, and dining area all flow around one central pillar and are distinguished by crisp touches of Victorian trim. Antiques

Left, above, the beautifully restored White House, with its traditional red tin roof, has four guest rooms. Below, the invitingly decorated sitting room.

mix with rattan furnishings in the floral living room, with big picture windows looking out to the lush garden.

Emanating from these common areas are four bedrooms, each with a different color theme. One particularly handsome bedroom features blue and white striped fabrics against a background of white walls and white wicker furnishings. An eclectic collection of books are displayed among two walls of built-in bookshelves.

Breakfast is a memorable occasion at Haikuleana. The gourmet entrées might include banana crêpes (made with homegrown bananas) or a glazed oven omelet baked with raw Hawaiian sugar and sprinkled with chopped macadamia nuts and coconut. Served in the dining room, each plate is creatively arranged with fresh fruit.

HAIKULEANA BED & BREAKFAST PLANTATION STYLE, 555 Haiku Road, Haiku, Maui, HI 96780-9607; (808) 575-2890; Dr. Frederick J. Fox, Jr., owner; Allyn R. Gardner, manager. Four rooms, all with private baths. Rates: $65 to $80, single; $80 to $95, double, including full gourmet breakfast. Children 7 or over permitted; no pets; no smoking; Swedish spoken; no credit cards. World-renowned windsurfing and surfing less than two miles away at Hookipa Beach. Shopping in nearby Paia and Makawao. Mama's Fish House, Haliimaile General Store, and Crossroads Cafe recommended for dining.

DIRECTIONS: from Kahului Airport, follow Rte. 36 toward Hana. Proceed through Paia to the 11-mile marker and turn right at Haiku Rd. Continue 1.1 miles to where the road forks into a "Y". B&B is on the left side of this intersection.

COUNTRY GARDEN COTTAGE

An enchanted cottage

Across the street from Bloom Cottage is another enchanting B&B called Country Garden Cottage. Also adjacent to the hosts' home, Country Garden has an earthier exterior of dark wood shingles and lava rock fireplace. Inside, however, it is anything but earthy.

The entire cottage was gutted and redesigned into a sparkling B&B by host Barbara Wimberly's architect husband. The beamed ceilings and walls have been painted in fresh cottage white, accented by soft green trim and green floral furnishings. Delicate pieces of starched lace and gauzy white curtains complete the light-infused effect. Everything is pristine, with the scent of potpourri in the air.

In the living room a pretty loveseat is placed before the fireplace on the polished wood floors. A full kitchen is incorporated into this same room, its refrigerator stocked with breakfast provisions that include homebaked items such as orange-date muffins and poppy seed bread. The bedroom, also in white and pale green, faces the rose garden. In the closet are plush terry robes.

Outside, the private lanai is enclosed by ferns and flowers, with one of the four resident cats usually stretched out in the sun. The surrounding garden features some of the most unusual hibiscus flowers on Maui (compliments of the original owner, a sea captain, who brought back many plants from his world travels). Higher on the hill, a second cottage is being built among the avocado trees. Called the Ivy Wood Cottage, it will be a smaller version of the Country Cottage, with the added feature of a whirlpool bath.

At this three thousand-foot elevation, nights are cool. Remember to bring warm clothes—hard as it is to believe, you'll need them!

Definitely a country garden.

A charming guest room—light and airy.

COUNTRY GARDEN COTTAGE BED & BREAKFAST, RR2 Box 224-A Kula Highway, Kula, Maui, HI 96790; (808) 878-2858; Barbara Wimberly, owner. One-bedroom cottage with kitchen and private bath; accommodates up to four persons. Second cottage scheduled for completion January, 1995. Rates: $90, double, including self-serve *aloha* breakfast; $10 for each additional person. Children welcome (babysitting services offered); no pets (4 outdoor cats on premises); no smoking; no credit cards. Tedeschi Winery, hiking on Haleakala, and Kula Botanical Gardens nearby.

DIRECTIONS: located in Keokea between Kula and Ulapalakua.

One of two immaculate guest rooms.

PILIALOHA BED & BREAKFAST COTTAGE

A cottage in a rose garden

Pilialoha means "friendship" in Hawaiian, and that is clearly how hosts Bill and Machiko Heyde wish to treat their guests. Machiko, who maintains an impeccable guest cottage adjacent to their home, is just about the sweetest, most charming hostess you could possibly find.

Set in the semi-rural area of upcountry Haiku, Pilialoha is posed at the upper end of a long, sloping lawn and manicured gardens. The two-acre property is bordered by old eucalyptus trees while the driveway is lined with Machiko's one hundred, carefully nurtured rose bushes—all individually labeled. An old-fashioned swing hangs from a tree just outside the cottage, overlooking the tranquil slope.

Serenely appointed in white and soft green, the living room and two bedrooms are cheery and immaculate, with views of the surrounding greenery from all the picture windows. Machiko has brought nature inside with various arrangements of fresh-cut roses and tropical flowers. Her hand-painted, quilted pillows and patchwork quilt are a perfect match with the prevailing tones of soft green.

But it's the attention to detail that really sets Pilialoha apart. The kitchen is fully equipped with all modern amenities, including a dishwater. And in the private carport you'll find a washer and dryer, plus complimentary beach equipment. Among the other thoughtful touches found throughout the cottage: a video about Maui for first-time visitors; a

The impeccable guest cottage.

cassette guide that guests can borrow for their trip to Hana; a coffee thermos for early morning visits to Haleakala Crater; and even postage stamps on the writing desk. "If the guests are from Canada, I add extra postage," says Machiko.

Pilialoha serves as a good central base for exploring the whole island. The closest town is Makawao, an interesting cowboy-artist village where you'll find more health food stores per square foot than anywhere on Maui.

PILIALOHA BED & BREAKFAST COTTAGE, 2512 Kaupakalua Road, Haiku, Maui, HI 96708; (808) 572-1440; Fax (808) 572-4612; Bill and Machiko Heyde, owners. Two-bedroom cottage with full kitchen and private bath accommodates up to five persons. Rates: $85, single or double, including self-serve continental plus breakfast; $10 for each additional person. Two-night minimum. Children accepted; no pets (one cat on premises); smoking allowed outside only; Japanese spoken. Hiking and windsurfing nearby. On the way to Hana and Haleakala National Park. Haliimaile General Store, Casanova Italian Restaurant, and Polli's Mexican Restaurant recommended for dining.

DIRECTIONS: from Kahului Airport, follow Hwy. 37 toward Haleakala. After the 7-mile marker, turn left on Makawao Ave. (Hwy. 365) and proceed through Makawao town. At the intersection of Kokomo Rd., Makawao Ave. becomes Kaupakalua Rd. Entrance to Pilialoha is .7 mile from that intersection, on the left.

Hanalei Bay with the fantastic beach that accounts for one-third of Bed, Breakfast and Beach's name (pages 64–65).

KAUAI

The natural beauty and mystical serenity of Kauai are enough to turn anyone into an incurable romantic. Despite the devastation caused in 1992 by Hurricane Iniki, the vegetation and beaches of the Garden Isle have almost returned to their former glory. And while many of the resort hotels still sit abandoned, the bed and breakfasts have bounced back with amazing resiliency—some better than ever.

Kauai B&B hosts usually advise first-time visitors to spend equal time on both sides of the island. This way they can experience the wide gamut of Mother Nature—from the dry climate and splendid beaches of Waimea and Poipu in the south, to the lush mountains and idyllic coves of Kilauea and Hanalei in the north.

Many B&B's are also clustered in the Wailua Homesteads, a residential area several miles inland from Kapaa. Centrally located, this pastoral valley makes a convenient base for exploring the entire island.

Hibiscus Cottage, a separate hideway in the garden.

KAY BARKER'S BED & BREAKFAST

A B&B with a loyal following

Kay Barker's may not be the most glamorous bed and breakfast on Kauai, but it's one of the best bargains for travelers on a budget. Despite its modest simplicity, this B&B has acquired a surprisingly loyal following over the past ten years.

Set in a semi-rural neighborhood of the Wailua Homesteads, the house has two living rooms, a dining area where breakfast is served, and a backyard lanai that faces the grazing cattle and pastoral slopes of Sleeping Giant Mountain.

Four bedrooms, each with patchwork quilts on their beds, are found inside the house. But without a doubt the most popular place to stay here is in the Hibiscus Cottage, a separate hideaway in the backyard. The one-bedroom cottage is quite cheerful and romantic, featuring a private lanai, kitchenette, and almost ethereal mountain view.

Left, above, view of Mt. Waialeale from a trail near the B&B. Below, the Orchid Room, one of four guest rooms in the main house.

Mornings are the best time for a hike up to the top of Sleeping Giant Mountain. (A wide path runs right from the house.) Even from the lower slopes you will be rewarded by a splendid vista across miles of highland valley pastures to Mount Waialeale, one of the wettest spots on earth.

Gordon Barker, who took over the B&B after Kay, his mother, passed away, has a cantankerous sense of humor that grows on you. Not only does he fix a terrific breakfast, but he will even wash your laundry! There aren't a lot of rules here, and at night Gordon leaves you free run of the house since he lives nearby.

One guest wrote in the comment book: "This was the best deal for my money I've ever gotten in my life."

KAY BARKER'S BED & BREAKFAST, P.O. Box 740, Kapaa, Kauai, HI 96746; (800) 835-2845; (808) 822-3073; Gordon Barker, host. Four rooms in main house, plus one separate cottage; all with private baths. Rates: $35 to $60, single; $45 to $70, double, including generous continental breakfast. Children welcome; local pets okay; smoking allowed; "broken English" spoken; Visa/MasterCard. Hiking trail right outside the door; Wailua River, Fern Grotto tours, golf, and swimming nearby. The Bull Shed and Kapaa Fish and Chowder recommended for dining in Kapaa.

DIRECTIONS: from Lihue Airport, follow Hwy. 56 north. Proceed to Hwy. 580 (just after crossing the Wailua River) and turn left. Continue up the hill for about 3 miles to Hwy. 581 (Kamalu Rd.) and turn right. Drive 1¾ miles to Lokelani Rd. and turn right. Turn right on Crossley Rd., then left on Ki'inani Pl. Kay Barker's is the big yellow house on the right.

The lily pond is the work of the owner—a landscaper.

The thatched cottage in the garden.

ROSEWOOD BED & BREAKFAST

Exotic gardens

This century-old former macadamia nut plantation home has been restored to look almost like new, in fresh yellow paint with white trim. The gardens surrounding the house—designed by owner Norbert Smith, a professional landscaper—are quite wonderful, with a profusion of tropical flowers, lily ponds, and trickling waterfalls.

There are a wide variety of accommodations here: The main house, which is nicely decorated in Laura Ashley and Waverly fabrics, has three bedrooms. The west-facing room on the second floor overlooks a huge avocado tree and has a pink-tiled tub for two. (Honeymoon and anniversary couples are given plumeria blossoms to float in the tub.) Another room is a not-too-private sun porch that is screened in on three sides. ("If you've come from New York and a blizzard, this is the place to be," says Norbert's wife, Rosemary.) But considering that the

Left, above, the Victorian Cottage, which closely resembles the main house. Below, chintz and other patterns enliven the living room in the main house.

main house is rather bustling with a still-active family life (one of their six children still lives at home and the others are often about), the two separate cottages in back appear to be more private choices.

One cottage—the "Victorian"—resembles the main house in miniature, sporting the same yellow-with-white trim and dormer windows. The interior features warm oak floors, crisp Laura Ashley-style décor, and sunlight streaming in from the high ceiling skylights. Breakfast provisions are left in the kitchen refrigerator.

Nestled in the trees on the far side of the yard is the Thatched Cottage, which looks like the original "little grass shack." The authentic thatched roof is steeply slanted, giving the cottage a cozy, tropical feel.

ROSEWOOD BED & BREAKFAST, 872 Kamalu Road, Kapaa, Kauai, HI 96746; (808) 822-5216; Fax (808) 822-5478; Norbert and Rosemary Smith, owners. Three rooms in main house with private baths, a one-bedroom thatched cottage, a two-bedroom Victorian cottage, and a hostel-style bunkhouse. Rates: $35 to $95; including continental breakfast for all but those in the bunkhouse. Children welcome; no pets; no smoking; German spoken; no credit cards. Four miles from beaches, shopping, theatre, and water sports. Restaurant Kintaro and A Pacific Cafe recommended for dining in Kapaa.

DIRECTIONS: from Lihue Airport, follow Rte. 56 north to Kapaa. Immediately after crossing the Wailua River Bridge, turn left at Hwy. 580 (Kuamoo Rd.). Proceed almost 3 miles past Opaekaa Falls and turn right on Hwy. 581 (Kamalu Rd.). House is on the right with a long, white picket fence.

Hosts Connie and Major with one of their adored cats.

Front exterior of the guest house.

INN PARADISE

A menagerie of friendly pets

Connie and Major, the hosts at this B&B, are a loving, spirited couple who have surrounded themselves with a literal paradise. Situated on three verdant acres in the Wailua Homesteads, their home and guest cottage overlook a slope of manicured grounds that are impeccably maintained by Major. Grass runs luxuriously down the hill to a fertile garden of pineapples, herbs, banana and papaya trees, while their two horses graze peacefully in a nearby pasture.

Three immaculate, wicker-furnished suites are found inside the guest house, their sliding glass doors opening onto a common lanai. Also provided are welcome fruit baskets and refrigerators stocked with breakfast in kitchens that range from small to full-sized.

Outside, you will most certainly meet Connie and Major's menagerie of friendly pets: In addition to the two horses, they also have five cats, one dog, three chickens that lay blue eggs, and three colorful parrots. Romeo and Juliet, a funny pair of yellow-naped Amazons, love to wow the guests with their five hundred-word vocabulary. You never know what they'll say next. Says Major: "They can even sing 'Rudolph the Red-Nosed Reindeer' and 'Old Mac-Donald Had A Farm.'

Ever gracious hosts, Connie and Major always greet their guests with a warm hug. After twenty-seven years of marriage, they still act like happy honeymooners. When not attending to their guests, they are often found riding their horses or tootling about in their antique roadster. During holidays they pull out all the stops, staging giant Easter egg hunts or cooking turkey in their Hawaiian-style *imu* for Thanksgiving. One guest put it aptly when she wrote: "We feel that the beauty and the magic of this whole island almost compares to the beauty and love that generates from you two people!"

INN PARADISE, Wailua Homesteads, Kauai; *represented by Hawaii's Best Bed & Breakfasts;* (800) 262-9912; (808) 885-4550. Three suites: two with one bedroom and one with two bedrooms; all with private baths. Rates: $50 to $85, including continental self-serve breakfast (2-night minimum). Children over 8 welcome; no pets (there are plenty in residence); smoking allowed on veranda only; no credit cards. Hiking at Keahua Arboretum, Kuilau Ridge trail (one of the most visually rewarding trails on the island), and Sleeping Giant trail nearby. The King and I recommended for dining in Kapaa.

DIRECTIONS: sent prior to departure.

Left, the horse pasture on the inn's grounds.

Breakfast in one of the suites.

MAKANA INN

A honeymoon cottage for two

This private cottage enjoys a serene setting at the end of a country road in the Wailua Homesteads. With its picturesque view of rolling pastures and waterfalls cascading from distant Mount Waialeale, Makana Inn is ideal for romantic couples. (Indeed, numerous proposals have taken place here.) Honeymooners are presented with leis and champagne by Sally and Jamie, the cheerful, handsome hosts who live next door.

Sally has decorated the sunny cottage with an artful eye in a most pleasing island style: Against the polished wood floors and whitewashed walls are a rainbow of fresh tropical colors—bold floral fabrics, vases of exotic flowers, and collectibles that possess a touch of both East and West. Her keen sense of taste is present in everything from the perfumed flowers in the bathroom to her antique Chinese needlework on the living room wall. An

Left, Birds of Paradise are just some of the tropical flowers that decorate the cottage.

The deck of the cottage overlooks a green pasture where the hosts' beloved horses graze peacefully.

Breakfast in the living room.

The colorful guest room.

armoire with an unusual grillwork of pineapples— the symbol of hospitality—disguises the television. A generous basket of tropical fruit and Sally's hot-from-the-oven bread are brought by the night before, while the pretty wicker breakfast table is already set.

The cottage and its small deck overlook a green pasture where Sally's Arabian and two prized quarterhorses graze. Her love of horses is no less equal to her love of Kauai, which she and Jamie first discovered while on honeymoon from San Diego. Tells Sally: "We took one look and said, 'We're moving!' "

After their larger house was blown away by Hurricane Iniki, this cottage served as Sally and Jamie's home for more than a year during the rebuilding. The Makana Inn has just recently reopened as a B&B.

MAKANA INN, Wailua Homesteads, Kauai; *represented by Hawaii's Best Bed & Breakfasts;* (800) 262-9912; (808) 885-4550. One-bedroom cottage with kitchen and private bath. Rates: $95, including self-serve continental breakfast (2-night minimum). Children welcome; no pets; smoking limited to outside areas; no credit cards. Sunday polo picnics on the north shore provide a unique local experience. A Pacific Cafe and The King and I recommended for dining in Kapaa.

DIRECTIONS: sent prior to departure.

The Pineapple Room is distinguished by a round bed.

Extensive landscaping at the front is visually striking.

Their airy living room is attractively appointed, with floors of koa and marble, a saltwater aquarium, and collection of Polynesian artifacts and paintings. Emanating from this are three bedrooms and a dining room where breakfast is served. A wall of French doors open to a long slate lanai that provides unbroken vistas of grass and sea.

Each of the bedrooms are named after a different fruit. The Pineapple Room is the biggest kick, with its goofy collection of pineapples and seven-foot round bed. ("This way, you never get up on the wrong side of bed," jokes Toby.) This room also has a nice marble bath and view of the distant ocean.

The "House of Rest" ("And I don't get any," quips Toby) is the type of homestay B&B where you'll feel like one of the family. Guests have free use of the whole house, including the kitchen.

HALE HO'O MAHA

Hosted by a dynamic duo

Hale Ho'o Maha (meaning "House of Rest") is a single-story modern home that sits on five green acres near Kilauea, on Kauai's north shore. Above a wide expanse of luxurious grass one can see a thin strip of the nearby blue Pacific.

Hosts Kirby and Toby are a fun-loving couple who have thoroughly immersed themselves in island life. Toby, a certified diver, will clue you in on the best secret underwater sites and beaches of Kauai. Kirby is a dynamic lady who enjoys dancing the hula and making leis (which she will demonstrate for guests if they are interested). She has also ridden in—and once won—the prestigious Pa'u Parade, held on special Hawaiian holidays. In the hallway are photos of Kirby sitting proudly on horseback, swathed in yards of purple satin and leis.

Left, above, the living room. Below, the Mango Room.

HALE HO'O MAHA, P.O. Box 422, Kilauea, Kauai, HI 96754; (800) 851-0291; (808) 828-1341; Kirby Guyer and Toby Searles, hosts. Three rooms: one with private bath and two with shared bath. Rates: $55 to $70, including continental breakfast. Children over 12 welcome; no pets; smoking permitted; Spanish spoken; Visa/MasterCard. Swimming, surfing, snorkeling, kayaking, biking, and hiking nearby.

DIRECTIONS: from Lihue Airport, follow Hwy. 56 north through Kapaa and just past Kilauea town. After the 24-mile marker, turn left at Kahiliholo Rd. (where a stone sign says "Kalihiwai Ridge"). Drive ¼ mile to 4646 Kahiliholo Rd.

BED, BREAKFAST AND BEACH

A world-class beach

Hosts Carolyn Barnes, left, and Diane Oliver at breakfast on the lanai.

Hanalei Bay is quite simply one of the most stunning spots on earth. Used as the setting for several movies, including "South Pacific," the lush, undulating mountains form a magnificent backdrop to the tranquil bay and its long crescent of soft sand beach. As you drive around that final bend in the north shore road and encounter your first full sight of Hanalei, the scene will be forever etched in your mind.

You can't stay any closer to Hanalei Bay than at Bed, Breakfast and Beach. Situated in the town of Hanalei, this contemporary three-story home is in a beachy residential neighborhood just one block from the water. A second-floor lanai wraps around the entire house, providing a partial ocean view and spectacular mountain panorama.

The gathering areas—a country-style living room with beamed ceilings, and the lanai—revolve around the second floor, whereas the guest quarters are scattered in various levels of the house. Of the four bedrooms (each varying widely in its level of privacy), the Bali Hai Suite is by far the most popular, especially for honeymooners. Encompassing the whole top floor in an unusual layout, the suite has an abundance of windows that boast three hundred-sixty-degree views.

The proximity of this B&B to the beach proves an irresistible lure. After a morning swim in the silky warm water and invigorating rinse in the B&B's outdoor shower, guests are greeted with fruit smoothies on the lanai. Breakfast might include cinnamon bread or pancakes, complemented by homemade coconut, guava or banana-flavored syrups.

Left, a corner of the sitting room.

The beautiful beach at Hanalei Bay near the inn (see also pages 52–53).

BED, BREAKFAST AND BEACH, P.O. Box 748, Hanalei, Kauai, HI 96714; (808) 826-6111; Carolyn Barnes, owner. Four rooms, all with private baths. Rates: $65 to $90, including extended continental breakfast; $15 for each additional person. Inquire about children; no pets; smoking allowed outside only; German spoken; no credit cards. Na Pali hike and all water sports, including river canoeing, nearby. Zodiac boat tours of the Na Pali coast depart right from the Hanalei Bay pier. Six eating establishments within walking distance.
DIRECTIONS: 150 yards from Hanalei Bay Beach Park. Directions given upon confirmation.

Hosts Ruth and Herb Bockleman.

The inn as it looks from the golf course.

HALE 'AHA

A custom-designed bed and breakfast

This lovely home was custom-designed by Herb and Ruth Bockleman especially to accommodate bed and breakfast guests. For instance, there are no adjoining walls between each of the five guest rooms and suites, providing the ultimate in peace and quiet. Among other modern comforts are televisions, kitchenettes, plush bathrooms, and private lanais.

Set in the exclusive Princeville resort community, Hale 'Aha (meaning "House of Gathering") has a panoramic view of the Hanalei mountains, the nearby ocean, and the Makai golf course. In fact, the fairway and sixth hole are right outside the back door, which makes an entertaining show from the lounge chairs on the lanai.

The whole house, including the common living room, is decorated in light pastel florals. Each of the guest rooms are spotless and spacious—especially the Penthouse Suite, which encompasses the whole top floor and has picture windows overlooking Hanalei's famous Bali Hai peaks. Cathedral ceilings make this suite appear even bigger than its thousand square feet.

Left, Makai golf course seen from the inn.

Herb and Ruth, a lovely retired couple, are the sweetest of hosts, and they treat their guests with lots of loving care. For dinner they will direct you to a number of fine restaurants in Princeville. The entire development is built on a bluff overlooking Hanalei Bay, so some of the nearby dining establishments—especially the Princeville Hotel—enjoy dazzling views.

In addition to golfing buffs, Herb and Ruth get their fair share of hikers, many of them bound for the famous Na Pali coast (only accessible by foot). One of Herb's most robust "hiker breakfast specials" includes steamed brown rice with raisins, served with a selection of fruit toppings freshly picked from Hale 'Aha's very own trees.

Bedroom of the Penthouse Suite.

HALE 'AHA, 3875 Kamehameha Rd., P.O. Box 3370, Princeville, Kauai, HI 96722; (800) 826-6733; (808) 826-6733; Herb and Ruth Bockleman, owners-hosts. Four rooms, including two suites, all with private baths (some with whirlpool tubs). Rates: $85 to $210, including hearty continental breakfast. Three-night minimum. No children; no pets; smoking allowed outside only; Visa/MasterCard. Guests receive discounts at Prince and Makai Golf Courses. Weekly and daily memberships available at Prince Health Club and Spa. Horseback riding, beaches, hiking trails, tennis courts, and shopping nearby. Bali Hai and La Cascata recommended for dining.

DIRECTIONS: from Lihue Airport, follow Hwy. 56 north towards Hanalei. Proceed for 30 miles to Princeville Resort entrance. Turn right, pass the guard gate, and turn right again on Kamehameha Rd.

WAIMEA PLANTATION COTTAGES

Vintage plantation cottages restored

This is truly an extraordinary place: Fifty-two plantation workers' homes have been faithfully restored and set amidst a gigantic coconut grove and oceanfront grounds that cover over 650 marvelous acres.

All of the vintage cottages, dating from 1886 to the 1930s, are classic examples of Hawaiian plantation architecture, distinguished by their tin roofs and wooden porches. Some still have signs that identify the original occupants. Ranging considerably in size (the largest is a five-bedroom Manager's Estate), even the smallest cottages have an airy feel, enhanced by an abundance of windows, ceiling fans, and shady lanais. Although they may at first appear somewhat spartan inside, it's more an atmosphere of minimalist luxury that prevails. Douglas fir floors, full kitchens, and period furnishings of koa, mahogany, and wicker are standard fare, as are all modern amenities. The lightweight, tropical, Hilo-designed bed linens couldn't be more suitable here.

The large pool augments the plantation's beach.

One could spend a whole afternoon just roaming the tranquil, expansive grounds. The cottages have been spread well apart in a series of long rows with broad "courtyards" of grass running to the sea. Nearly six hundred towering coconut trees, monumental banyan trees, and tropical flowers add to the already idyllic setting. Next to an endless stretch of black sand beach (near where Captain Cook first landed during his discovery of the Hawaiian Islands) are tennis courts and an inviting pool.

In the century-old main building (filmed in "The Thornbirds" series) The Grove restaurant offers three meals a day.

Left, one of the original tin-roofed cottages.

WAIMEA PLANTATION COTTAGES, 9600 Kaumualii Highway. #367, Waimea, Kauai, HI 96796; (800) 9-WAIMEA; (808) 338-1625; Ray Blouin, general manager. Fifty-two cottages ranging from one to five bedrooms, all with private baths. Rates: $90 to 150 for one-bedroom cottages; $120 to $225 for two to four-bedroom cottages; $350 for five-bedroom Manager's Estate; 3-night minimum. Breakfast packages available. Children welcome (lots of chickens and horses to feed, plus a children's pool); no pets; smoking allowed on lanais only; Japanese and Filippino spoken; all credit cards accepted. Swimming, horseshoes, volleyball, croquet, horseback riding (at adjacent stables), and tennis on grounds. Polihale, Salt Pond Beach, Kokee State Park, and Waimea Canyon nearby. Toi's Thai Kitchen, Green Garden, Hanapepe Book Store, and The Grove recommended for dining.

DIRECTIONS: from Lihue Airport, take Hwy. 50 southwest for 27 miles to Waimea town. Two blocks west of Waimea Canyon Dr., turn left into the gravel driveway of the front office.

The cottage bedrooms are simple but comfortable.

VICTORIA PLACE

Gardenia-scented poolside breakfasts

It's no wonder that Edee Seymour was awarded the 1992 Aloha Spirit Award from the Kauai Chamber of Commerce. Not only is she extremely hospitable to her B&B guests, but for over a year Edee also opened her doors to people left homeless by Hurricane Iniki. This outgoing woman has an obvious love of people and passion for Kauai.

Located in a quiet residential area just minutes from Koloa and Poipu Beach, Victoria Place is a private home where each guest room has its own entry. Several narrow bedrooms—each with tropical décor and fresh orchids—are lined closely together by the swimming pool, while the fourth—called Victoria's Other Secret—offers considerably more privacy and space in a downstairs wing of the house. This much-requested studio apartment also has a loft and its own kitchenette.

The sunny, high-ceilinged living room provides

Left, above, host Edee Seymour (standing) at breakfast. Below, the garden pool.

A shell collection makes an interesting coffee table in the living room.

a well-stocked "Kauai library" and wonderful collection of shells. From here, sliding doors open to a lanai which looks across the jungled hills and cane fields to Poipu Beach in the distance. The swimming pool, surrounded by a colorful wall of gardenias, hibiscus and shell ginger, is another pleasant spot to relax.

Guests sometimes take a morning swim before gathering at the poolside breakfast table where Edee holds court. Along with exotic fruits from the local farmer's market, she serves a variety of yummy toppings—granola, coconut, yogurt, guava butter, and lime squeezes. After a day of sightseeing, hiking or sunbathing at Poipu Beach, guests return to find Edee with a bowl of popcorn and refreshments in hand. She loves to chat with her guests and can steer them to little-known spots on the island.

Shell ginger grows in the garden.

VICTORIA PLACE, 3459 Lawai Loa Lane, Koloa, Kauai, HI 96756; (808) 332-9300; Edee Seymour, hostess. Four rooms, one a separate studio, all with private baths. (One room designed for physically disabled guests.) Rates: $55, single; $65 to $75, double, $95 studio, including continental plus breakfast. No children under 15; no pets; smoking allowed outside only; no credit cards. Poipu Beach and golf course nearby. Hiking trails right outside the door. Kalaheo Steak House, Hanapepe Book Store & Expresso Bar (for vegetarian), and Fisherman's Galley recommended for dining.

DIRECTIONS: from Lihue Airport, take Hwy. 50 southwest for about 15 miles. Turn left at Hwy. 530, proceed 1.3 miles to Lawai Loa Lane, (marked by a green and white-striped pole), and turn right.

POIPU PLANTATION

Heavenly beaches

Poipu Plantation, a family-owned complex, is divided into two types of accommodations: In front is a plantation-style bed and breakfast house; to the rear is a collection of non-B&B rental units. And from their check-in office the owners also operate a statewide reservation service.

Aside from breakfast time, which is served by owner Evie Warner or manager Chris, guests otherwise have the house to themselves during the day. Among the common rooms is a screened, white wicker-filled lanai that is bright and cheery. From here you can see over the residential rooftops to the blue-blue ocean, a short walk away. The adjoining living room, also with ocean views and wicker furnishings, is stocked with coffee table books, a television and VCR. Elsewhere on the grounds are a hot tub and barbecue that all the Poipu Plantation guests are welcome to use.

The three pristine, uncluttered bedrooms feature floral spreads, wicker furnishings, and larger-than-usual bathrooms. Only one—the master bedroom—has an ocean view, while the other two bedrooms face a garden.

Life here revolves around the nearby beaches. Indeed, the neighborhood seems to be an equal mix of private homes and vacation rentals. Although the sand is still recovering here and there from the hurricane, some of the island's best swimming beaches, including the popular Poipu Beach Park, are just down the hill.

Flowers everywhere.

POIPU PLANTATION, 1792 Pe'e Road, Koloa, Kauai, HI 96756; (800) 733-1632; (808) 742-7038; Evie Warner, owner; Christine Fonzi, manager. Three rooms with private bath (plus nine non-B&B rental units). Rates: $70 to $75, including continental *aloha* breakfast. Children over 10 welcome in B&B (private units are available for younger children); no pets; smoking allowed outside only; Visa/MasterCard/American Express. Brennecke's Beach, Shipwreck Beach (both for experienced swimmers only), and Poipu Beach Park are all within several blocks. Many fine restaurants nearby.

DIRECTIONS: from Lihue Airport, follow Hwy. 50 southwest to Koloa-Poipu turnoff at Hwy. 520 and turn left. Proceed into Koloa until the road ends at Koloa Rd. Turn right, then left on Poipu Rd. Turn right on Hoowili Rd., then left on Hoone Rd. which becomes Pe'e Rd.

Left, Poipu Beach in the distance viewed from the proximity of the plantation.

The breakfast lanai.

Hot tub in the garden.

The stunning two-story living-dining room.

The Punana Aloha Room with its willow canopied bed.

GLORIA'S SPOUTING HORN BED & BREAKFAST

An awesome ocean setting

After Hurricane Iniki swept this entire bed and breakfast out to sea, Gloria and Bob Merkle rebuilt their home into a beautiful fortress. The foundation is now solidly anchored with deep, pier-sized pilings. Visible from the three-story living room are open ceiling trusses made of steel. "Some people think this is overkill," says Gloria, "but at least we'll *never* blow away again."

Starting from scratch also enabled the Merkles to re-design their home as a better-than-ever B&B with luxurious amenities. For example, every guest room now has a wet bar and microwave; each bathroom features a deep soaking tub, separate shower, and changing area; a refreshing breeze is circulated by multiple walls of bedroom window shutters.

The whole house smells of the fresh country pine

Left, above, newly rebuilt after the hurricane, the striking new building faces out to sea. Below, host Gloria Merkle.

woodwork which lines the interior. Each bedroom is spanking new and pleasingly appointed. The "Punana Aloha" Room (meaning "Love Nest") is especially unique, with its full canopy willow bed and rustic, handcrafted furnishings.

As the only oceanfront B&B on Kauai, Gloria's takes full advantage of its terrific setting. The long balconies outside each bedroom offer sensational views of the surf pounding on the rocks. Down the coast you can even see Spouting Horn, a natural sea geyser which sprays up to forty feet in the air.

The breakfast buffet, served on the lanai, includes such treats as macadamia nut coffee, guava juice, tropical fruits, a baked entrée, and perhaps crusty Cuban or Irish soda bread.

GLORIA'S SPOUTING HORN BED & BREAKFAST, 4464 Lawai Beach Road, Koloa, Kauai, HI 96756; (808) 742-6995; Gloria and Bob Merkle, owners. Three oceanfront rooms with lanais and private baths. Rates: $125 to $150, including extended continental breakfast. Three-night minimum. No children under 14; no pets; no smoking indoors; no credit cards. Fishing, golf, tennis, helicoptering, whale watching, and all water sports at Poipu Beach nearby. Weddings can also be arranged here, and Bob, a licensed minister, will even perform the ceremony. Beach House and Brennecke's located nearby for dining.

DIRECTIONS: from Lihue Airport, follow Hwy. 50 southwest to Koloa-Poipu turnoff at Hwy. 520 (also known as the Tree Tunnel). Turn left here, continuing into Koloa. Turn right at Koloa Rd., then left at Poipu Rd. At the "Welcome to Poipu" sign, take the right fork, which is Lawai Rd., and proceed 1.5 miles.

Overleaf, the captivating view from the lanai.

Poipu
Bed & Breakfast
Inn

742-1146

POIPU B&B INN

Dolphin and whale watching

Poipu Bed & Breakfast Inn, another top B&B on Kauai, consists of two delightful cottages, each about one block apart. The original cottage, built in 1933, is an enchanting pink confection, with white lattice trim and Victorian wicker complementing the old-fashioned lanai and common living room. Pine antiques and carousel horses—a penchant of owner Dotti Cichon — mingle nicely with soft tropical colors in the four guest rooms.

The second cottage, which is closer to the ocean, is slightly larger but with a similar layout—a pleasant lanai and gathering room from which numerous guest rooms emanate. The look here is a bit more contemporary and festively tropical. As in the vintage cottage, most of the bathrooms here are exceptionally luxurious, featuring state-of-the-art fixtures. In the Coral Room, which is a guest favorite, the huge whirlpool tub and separate shower spring straight from the pages of *Architectural Digest*.

The newer cottage sits across the street from Koloa Landing, once the third busiest whaling port in Hawaii. The sealife, both above and below the water, is still incredibly active here. Guests are treated to frequent dolphin and whale shows from the lanai. From each bedroom you can hear the waves breaking on the rocks.

Breakfast—beautifully arranged exotic fruits and breads garnished with flowers from the surrounding garden—is served on the lanai of the ocean-facing cottage, so guests from the other cottage stroll down the road to gather here each morning.

Left, above, the living room of the 1930s Cottage. Below, the 1930s Cottage itself.

POIPU BED & BREAKFAST INN, 2720 Hoonano Road, Poipu Beach, Kauai, HI 96756; (800) 22-POIPU; (808) 742-1146; Dotti Cichon, owner. Nine rooms in two cottages, all with private baths; some rooms with kitchenettes and whirlpool tubs for two. One room is handicapped accessible. Rates: $110 to $175, including tropical continental breakfast; $15 surcharge for a one-night stay. Afternoon tea and breakfast in bed available. Children welcome; no pets; no smoking; French and German spoken; all credit cards accepted. Poipu Beach is two blocks away. Free guest privileges at the Kiahuna Tennis Club included. Whale watching (Nov. to April), snorkeling, helicopter rides, boat tours, kayaking, and diving tours can be arranged. Koloa Broiler is a great local spot for dinner.

DIRECTIONS: from Lihue Airport, follow Hwy. 50 southwest to Koloa-Poipu turnoff at Hwy. 520. Turn left here, continuing into Koloa. Turn right on Koloa Rd., then left on Poipu Rd. At the "Welcome to Poipu" sign, take the right fork, which is Lawai Rd. Immediately veer left again on Hoonani Rd. The inn is the first house over the wooden bridge.

The Bougainvillea Room.

Aloha breakfast on the lanai.

Macadamia nuts in the shell.

The main house.

WINTERS MAC NUT FARM & INN

Fun on the farm

Have you ever seen hens that lay green eggs? Or mangosteens and rambutans? How would you like to learn—hands on, if you wish—how macadamia nuts are grown and harvested? These are only a few of the uncommon things you will experience at Winters Mac Nut Farm, a fun B&B in the Wailua Homesteads.

The farm actually consists of one large orchard where an assortment of fruit and nut trees grow. Although it started out as a one hundred-forty-tree macadamia nut grove, Hurricane Iniki wiped out all but six trees. Undaunted, owners Eileen and Dale Winters replanted new "mac nut" trees that will soon flourish again. In addition, they are now experimenting with little-known exotic fruits such as mangosteens and rambutans.

It's hard to believe that all this farming knowledge comes from a couple who moved here from Newport Beach, California. With a perpetual twinkle in her eye, Eileen approaches the whole venture with a wonderful sense of humor. She loves to surprise her guests by offering them green eggs for breakfast— the happy results of her Rhode Island Red hens. "I usually come down around five o'clock every day and have a glass of wine with 'the girls,' " she says, referring to her hen house.

With all the amusing farm antics going on, the actual accommodations seem almost secondary here. There are several rooms in the main house, plus a separate cottage, and a larger house in another neighborhood altogether. The cheerful cottage is most private and convenient to all the farm action— the main show here.

WINTERS MAC NUT FARM & INN, 6470 Makana Road, Kapaa, Kauai, HI 96746; (800) 572-8156; (808) 822-3470; Dale & Eileen Winters, owners-hosts. Two bedrooms in main house with one shared bath; one private guest house on the grounds; and a large house about one mile away on the cliff above the Wailua River. Rates: $50 to $125, including served *aloha* breakfast for guests in main house; self-serve breakfast in other houses; $10 for each additional person. Children welcome; no pets; smoking permitted; Spanish and Hawaiian spoken; Visa/MasterCard. Hiking, fishing, Fern Grotto tours, horseback riding, and Opaekaa Falls nearby. Charlie's Place and A Pacific Cafe recommended for dining in Kapaa.

DIRECTIONS: from Lihue Airport, follow Hwy. 56 north to Kapaa. Immediately after crossing the Wailua River Bridge, turn left at Hwy. 580 (Kuamoo Rd.). Proceed almost 3 miles past Opaekaa Falls to Hwy. 581 (Kamalu Rd.) and turn right. Turn left on Opaekaa Rd., then right on Makana Rd. Farmhouse is at the end of Makana Rd., to the right.

Host Eileen Winters with the green eggs.

MOLOKAI

St. Joseph's Church, across the street from Kamalo Plantation.

Molokai is old, authentic Hawaii. The least developed and populated of the five major islands, it is not for those who need a lot of activity. There are no shopping centers, movie theaters, or fast food chains. The biggest town on the island is about four blocks long. And who needs traffic signals when life is already in the slow lane?

As for scenic beauty, hiking, and communing with nature, Molokai has everything to offer. The dramatic sea cliffs of the Pali Coast (which you'll see as you fly in from Maui) are some of the highest in the world. And breathtaking Halawa Valley could serve as a backdrop for "Paradise Lost." If you're the one who is looking to get lost, allow at least a few days for this island.

The secluded guest cottage.

KAMALO PLANTATION

Utter tranquility

Situated on a five-acre tropical garden and lime orchard at the foot of Mount Kamakou, Kamalo Plantation is surrounded by abundant scenic beauty. Sometimes you can see up to seven waterfalls on the mountain. The ruins of an ancient *heiau* (sacred site) on the property only add to the sense of utter tranquility.

Accommodations include a simple, secluded cottage and two rooms in the main house. Though the cottage offers more privacy, many guests prefer the main house rooms, which are quite peaceful and pleasant. Like the rest of the house, they have an airy, somewhat Oriental look. One bedroom is uniquely designed with an entire wall missing—it is screened but otherwise open to the outdoors. The refreshing breeze that wafts through this room gives

Left, above, owners Glenn and Akiko Foster. Below, a guest room in the main house is occasionally host to Toots the cat.

one the illusion of being outdoors. At night, all you hear are the clicking of the geckos and the calling of wild axis deer. In the morning, the roosters provide your wake-up call.

Hosts Glenn and Akiko Foster, who have lived all over the world, discovered this home two years ago while on a sailing trip around the islands. Charming hosts, they welcome their guests with lots of nice touches such as homebaked cookies, a basket of just-picked limes, and iced tea in the room refrigerators. When not entertaining their guests with tales of local lore, they're usually out picking limes in their orchard. They have a bevy of friendly pets—two cats named Boots and Toots, three dogs who act as your official welcoming committee, and a Hawaiian pony that likes to follow guests on their jogs.

KAMALO PLANTATION, HC01, Box 300, Kaunakakai, Molokai, HI 96748; (808) 558-8236; Glenn and Akiko Foster, owners. One cottage with full kitchen and private bath; two rooms in the main house with shared bath (booked for only one group at a time). Rates: $55 to $75, including *aloha* breakfast. Two-night minimum in cottage. Children allowed in cottage; no pets (various resident pets on the premises); smoking allowed outside or on deck; German and Japanese spoken; no credit cards. Hiking, historic sites, sailing, ocean fishing, mountain biking, and horseback riding nearby. Hotel Molokai, Kualapuu Cookhouse, and Jo Jo's recommended for dining.

DIRECTIONS: from Molokai Airport, follow Hwy. 460 east to Kaunakakai. Continue east through town (the highway changes to Hwy. 450) and proceed 10.5 miles. The B&B is across the street from a small white church.

A breakfast fruit plate of papaya, orange, and lime.

Pool at Holualoa Inn (pages 118–119), showing Kona Bay in the distance.

HAWAII

The island of Hawaii is better known as the Big Island, and for good reason. Nearly twice the size of all the other islands combined, Hawaii boasts the greatest number of bed and breakfasts as well.

An amazing number of fine B&B's are situated around the two-store village of Volcano on the south side of the Big Island. At four thousand feet in elevation, the Volcano area is often cloaked in a cool mist. The prime attraction is Hawaii Volcanoes National Park, which takes a minimum of two or three days to explore. The continuous activity of Madam Pele, the fire goddess, is an exciting show of nature at its most primal.

The B&B's on the rest of the Big Island are as varied as the landscape. While the Hilo side is lush with waterfalls and tropical gardens, the Kona side is dry and sunny, with long stretches of stark, black lava rock. The northern ranch country of Waimea offers rolling pastoral scenery and the most delightful climate on the island. There are also some enchanting B&B's hidden in the coffee-scented coastal foothills of south Kona.

Brian and Lisha Crawford with Batman the dog and Ramona the chicken.

CHALET KILAUEA

Upcountry sophistication

Chalet Kilauea is a surprising haven of refinement in the rural Volcano upcountry. The main building, or chalet, is highlighted by an inviting, second-floor living room panelled in warm wood and tastefully appointed with leather couches, fascinating artwork, and treasures from all over the world. Guests are invited to help themselves to a huge CD listening library, play at the marble gaming table, or curl up with a good book in front of the fire.

Off the living room are three bedrooms inspired by African, Oriental and European themes. The fourth guest room—the Tree House Suite—is reached via a stairway from the outside deck. There are also several attractive rental cottages nearby.

Among the many luxuries you'll enjoy here are afternoon tea, welcome chocolates, fresh flowers, and plush terry robes for your dip in the hot tub.

The candlelit, gourmet breakfast is not to be missed. In an Art Deco-style breakfast room, tables are set with fine china, candles and linens. Accompanied by classical music, your first course begins with a bed of fresh fruit topped by a triple cream

Left, two striking public rooms used by guests.

CHALET KILAUEA—THE INN AT VOLCANO, P.O. Box 998, Volcano, HI 96785; (800) 937-7786; (808) 967-7786; Fax (808) 967-8660; Lisha and Brian Crawford, owners. Theme rooms, suites and vacation homes, all with private baths. Rates: $75 to $225, including a candlelit two-course full gourmet breakfast for B&B guests. Children allowed in vacation homes only; no pets; smoking allowed outdoors only; French, Dutch, Spanish and Portuguese spoken; all credit cards accepted. Hawaii Volcanoes National Park, golf course, helicopter rides, hiking, birdwatching and black sand beach nearby.

DIRECTIONS: from Hwy. 11, between 26 and 27-mile marker, turn down Wright Rd. (Rte. 148) and proceed $\frac{3}{4}$ mile.

The shingled inn and its landscaped grounds.

sauce and tropical fruit purée. The main course might include such creative dishes as Gujarati Indian Eggs with broiled tomatoes, Japanese eggs, or "Eggs in a Nest."

Behind all of these sophistications are owners Lisha and Brian Crawford, a poised and well-traveled young couple. After spending years touring the world, Lisha and Brian settled in Volcano and blithely transformed this slated-for-the-bulldozer property into a worldly haven. On top of their ongoing improvements, they also operate a statewide reservation service. Always in evidence are their quirky collection of little greeters: Cloe the cat, Batman the Pomeranian, and two exotic bantam chickens named Ramona and Snookums.

The Continental Lace Room.

HYDRANGEA COTTAGE

A veritable Shangri-La

The sitting room, warmed by a wood stove on cool nights.

Hydrangea Cottage is a veritable Shangri-La in a flower-filled, fern-forest setting. Nestled on an exclusive estate in the Volcano area, this romantic retreat offers the ultimate in privacy along with all the modern comforts of home.

You enter the grounds through an electronic gate and follow a winding, moss-covered driveway past rolling lawns that are landscaped with hydrangeas, cymbidium orchids, and hapuu tree ferns. The cottage is behind a large main house (called the Mountain House) which is also available to guests when the owners are not in residence. A genial caretaker greets you and discreetly vanishes once you're settled in.

Calling this a "cottage" is probably a misnomer, as it is more the size of a small house. There is a large living room, full kitchen, separate bedroom, and ample bathroom. A wall of windows and sliding doors run down the entire length of the cottage, looking out past a wraparound lanai to a sea of feathery ferns and ohia trees. Handsomely furnished, the cottage provides plenty of extra comforts—a wood-burning stove, breakfast provisions, complimentary sherry, beautiful sprays of fresh-cut orchids, a television, telephone, washer and dryer. With a shortage of restaurants in the Volcano area, the fully-equipped kitchen comes in handy.

There is an utter sense of seclusion here. Aside from the sound of soft night rains and exotic morning birds, all is absolutely quiet. Snuggled under your electric blanket and down comforter, you'll be assured a peaceful night's rest.

The Mountain House is a sumptuous option for executive or family retreats. Elegantly Oriental in décor, the huge home features no less than two living rooms, three bedrooms, and a spotless, state-of-the-art gourmet kitchen.

The gardens abound in delicate orchids.

Left, the grounds, showing Mauna Loa peeking through the clouds in the distance.

HYDRANGEA COTTAGE, Volcano; *represented by Hawaii's Best Bed & Breakfasts;* (800) 262-9912; (808) 885-4550. One-bedroom cottage and three-bedroom executive home on 3 acres, both with full kitchens, washers and dryers, and private baths. Rates: $110 for Hydrangea Cottage; $160 per couple for Mountain House, including self-serve continental breakfast (2-night minimum). Inquire about children over 6; no pets, no credit cards. Hawaii Volcanoes National Park, Volcano Winery, excellent hiking nearby. Kilauea Lodge recommended for dining.

DIRECTIONS: sent prior to departure.

Common room at Hale o Aloha building.

The restaurant building.

KILAUEA LODGE

Scandinavian country charm

Of the many bed and breakfasts in the Volcano area, the Kilauea Lodge draws the most attention. The main structure, which is actually the dining room, strikes an impressive sight from Old Volcano Road, with its wide front lawn, circular driveway, and flying flags. Its twelve rooms have the ambience of a luxurious mountain lodge and the restaurant happens to be one of the best on the island. Even if you're staying elsewhere in Volcano, you will probably wind up eating dinner here, as this is also about the only dining option in the area.

Built in 1938 for the YMCA, Hale o Aloha—as it was called then—was a ten-acre retreat for Hawaiian children exploring the volcano area. Albert and Lorna Jeyte bought and refurbished the various buildings in 1986. Lorna runs the inn with her staff while German-born chef Albert oversees the restaurant.

The guest quarters are disbursed among three buildings ranging in size from a single cottage to the new Hale o Aloha building, which has an inviting common room and fireplace. The bedrooms here have a sort of Scandinavian country charm, with warm wood panelling, beamed ceilings, lace

Left, the dining room.

KILAUEA LODGE AND RESTAURANT, P.O. Box 116, Volcano, HI 96785; (808) 967-7366; Albert and Lorna Jeyte, owners. Twelve rooms, all with private baths; some with fireplaces. Rates: $85 to $105, single; $90 to $125, double, including full breakfast. Children welcome; no pets; smoking limited; German spoken; Visa/MasterCard. Hawaii Volcanoes National Park, one mile away, offers hiking, birdwatching, and viewing of lava flow. Golf, helicopter rides, and winery nearby. Kilauea Lodge Restaurant is open nightly for dinner; reservations strongly recommended.

DIRECTIONS: from Hilo and Hwy. 11, turn right just past the 26-mile marker.

curtains, and simple comforters. Many of the bathrooms feature high ceilings and skylights. Through each window is a picture of lush greenery. The large honeymoon suite has a particularly nice view of the gardens from its private, second-floor balcony.

The Kilauea Restaurant still features its original, high-beamed ceilings and a huge lava rock fireplace—the Fireplace of Friendship—which is imbedded with memorabilia from its YMCA camp days. Pair this with Hawaiian prints, rattan chairs, tropical flowers, and a European-Hawaiian menu . . . and the results are an atmosphere like no other place.

Lorna and Albert Jeyte.

The exotically designed main house.

HALE OHIA COTTAGES

Lush, landscaped Oriental gardens

Built in 1931, this former summer estate is surrounded by several acres of exotic, Oriental-inspired gardens. Rolling carpets of grass mingle with sugi pines, camelias, azaleas, hydrangeas, and orchids. The ohia tree, which the B&B is named after, is also in abundance. Its lehua blossoms are believed to be sacred to Madame Pele, the volcano goddess.

The lovely main house, with its conical, red-roofed turret and multi-paned windows, contains one guest suite, while numerous adjacent cottages provide additional B&B accommodations. The cottages are simply furnished and somewhat reminiscent of mountain cabins. Indeed, at this four thousand-foot elevation, the winter temperatures can drop to under fifty degrees at night—cold by Hawaiian standards. The cottages are outfitted with heaters, some fireplaces, and electric blankets—a novelty for most islanders.

The Hale Lehua Cottage, with its lava rock fireplace and garden view, is a private and romantic favorite. The Ihilani Cottage is a brand new addition

Left, Hale Lehua Cottage in the opulently landscaped grounds.

to the grounds. Several other suites are found in the former gardener's cottage.

Behind the main house is a Japanese *furo*, or hot soaking tub. Big enough for two, it sits on the edge of a wooden deck that overlooks the tranquil gardens. Chairs are grouped here and there under the trees, offering little niches of serenity.

HALE OHIA COTTAGES, P.O. Box 758, Volcano, HI 96785; (800) 455-3803; (808) 967-7986; Michael Tuttle, proprietor. Five units, including three cottages, all with private baths. Main house available for weddings and receptions. Rates: $70 to $100, including self-serve breakfast; $15 for each additional person. Children welcome; no pets; smoking allowed outdoors only; all credit cards accepted. One mile from Hawaii Volcanoes National Park. Kilauea Lodge recommended for dining. Private chef can also be arranged.

DIRECTIONS: opposite Haunani Rd. on Hwy. 11 in Volcano Village.

The guest cottages are simply furnished.

Kahau a 'lea Room.

CARSON'S VOLCANO COTTAGE

Rustic cottages in the rain forest

Brenda and Tom Carson's collection of enchantingly rustic cottages are hidden deep in the Volcano rainforest. The fairytale-like garden they encircle is so lush that its sweet, damp scent fills the air.

The one private guest cottage, called Nick's Cabin 19, was built in 1946 as a mountain getaway. Roughly panelled in whitewashed wood, the cabin comprises one large room with a kitchen, two beds, and a wood stove. Across the garden is a larger cottage that is divided into three cozy bedrooms, each with its own private entrance. The Kahau a'lea ("land of the mist") Room is designed to transport you back to Princess Kailuani's era, with period antiques, layers of white lace on the bed, and old-fashioned, sepia-toned photos of the Hawaiian monarchy. Whereas this room is all neutral creams and browns, the Kau ("warm wind") Room is painted

Left, Nick's Cabin 19, with a wood stove, is one of several rustic cottages.

in hot tropical colors reminiscent of the Royal Hawaiian Hotel. The third room, Kobayashi ("small forest"), is named and designed in honor of the Japanese family that originally lived here.

Though their themes are varied, all the guest rooms have a kind of whimsical romance, enhanced by a nostalgic medley of 1930s and 40s fabrics—vintage Hawaiian curtains and pillows mixed with antique lace. Brenda's collection of Depression glass and old-fashioned tea cups are set at little breakfast tables in each room.

Brenda stresses that their B&B is for people who prefer privacy as there are no common areas besides the inviting hot tub in which to gather. Breakfast, placed in the refrigerator of each room the day before, includes a nicely arranged plate of cut tropical fruit and perhaps lox, bagels and cream cheese or microwaveable French toast.

CARSON'S VOLCANO COTTAGE, P.O. Box 503, Volcano, HI 96785; (808) 967-7683; Tom and Brenda Carson, owners. Three rooms and one cottage, all with private baths. Rates: $60 to $95, single; $70 to $105, double, including self-serve breakfast. Children allowed in private cottage only; no pets (two cats and a dog in residence); smoking allowed outdoors only; Visa/MasterCard/Discover. Hawaii Volcanoes National Park, Volcano Winery, and orchid gardens nearby.

DIRECTIONS: from Hilo Airport, follow Hwy. 11 to Volcano. After 25-mile marker turn left on Jade St., then right on 6th St. Proceed .6 mile. (6th St. will become a dirt road.)

MAUREEN'S BED & BREAKFAST

An aviary, pond, and Japanese garden

Hilo isn't likely the first place you'll think of spending Christmas, but Maureen's definitely sets one in the mood. The living room, or "great hall," of this B&B looks positively baronial with its high vaulted ceilings, dark redwood and cedar panelling, and hanging tapestries. During the holidays, innkeeper Maureen Goto fills the hall with a giant Christmas tree. But instead of biting winter cold, the open hall is filled with the balmy, tropical breezes of nearby Hilo Bay.

Originally known as the Saiki Mansion, the two-story home was built in 1932 by a Japanese banker and his Hawaiian wife. While raising their eight children they added many unique touches to the house, such as a double staircase in the great hall, arched windows and doorways, a tea room, and Japanese garden. By the time Maureen took it over, the mansion had fallen into complete disrepair. She is gradually breathing life back into it.

The former upstairs tea room is now a screened lanai-television room with a large aviary of twittering love birds and cockatiels. The Japanese garden and koi pond—flourishing with gardenias, bromiliads, jasmine, orchids, and torch ginger—have been restored to their former glory. And the great room is filled with old-fashioned furnishings that Maureen brought from her native East Coast. The bedrooms are somewhat modest in comparison.

The only real swimming beaches in Hilo are along this four-mile stretch of road which runs along the

The rear gardens.

south end of Hilo Bay. One block from Maureen's is Richardson's Ocean Park, which has a black sand beach. Across the street is the James Kealoha Beach Park, a great swimming spot that is protected from the waves by a breakwater.

MAUREEN'S BED & BREAKFAST, 1896 Kalanianaole Avenue, Hilo, HI 96720-4918; (808) 935-9018; Maureen Goto, owner. Five rooms, four with shared baths. Rates: $40, single; $60, double, including full breakfast. No children under age 7; no pets (resident dog on premises); smoking in designated area only; no credit cards. Swimming and snorkeling across the street. Harrington's, Royal Siam, and Cafe Pesto's recommended for dining.

DIRECTIONS: from Hilo Airport, turn right on Kanuelehua, then right on Kamehameha. Proceed 2.7 miles on Kamehameha, which becomes Kalanianaole Ave.

Left, the "Great Hall."

The Merrie Monarch Room.

James Kealoha Beach Park, where guests swim.

The Chinese Room, with 1836 Chinese chairs.

WAIPIO WAYSIDE BED & BREAKFAST INN

Set on a bluff above the ocean

The Waipio Valley, at the northern end of the Hamakua Coast, has long been considered the spiritual center of Hawaii. Filled with *heiaus* (sacred sites), waterfalls, and taro terraces, this glorious valley opens out to a mile-long black sand beach that can be reached only by foot or four-wheel drive.

Ten minutes away, the Waipio Wayside Bed & Breakfast Inn shares the same unspoiled atmosphere. Set on a thousand-foot bluff above the ocean, this 1938 plantation home was built in an East Coast cottage design, complete with white picket fence. Out back, a gazebo extends from the lanai, overlooking the sloping lawn and distant blue sea.

Owner Jacqueline Horne runs her B&B with the natural warmth of one born to be an innkeeper. She loves to cook and entertain while exuding a genuine love of her surroundings. Having moved here seven years ago from Northern California, Jackie finds the

Left, above, the Birds Eye Room. Below, Owner Jacqueline Horne.

Waipio area refreshingly "rural and old-fashioned—like California was when I was growing up." Her cozy B&B is filled with a combination of antiques, wicker and rattan, everything designed with relaxation in mind.

Of the five guest rooms, the Birds Eye Room is perhaps the most special. Paneled in light knotty pine from ceiling to floor, the bedroom radiates a warm glow. Double doors open directly onto the common lanai where a double hammock beckons.

Jackie, who is currently at work on a cookbook, whips up a full gourmet breakfast each morning, beginning with local Hamakua Coast coffee and fresh fruit smoothies. A typical entrée might include banana pancakes, potato soufflé, or quiche, and perhaps cranberry muffins or sour cream coffee cake. She also plies her guests with afternoon tea and yummy, homemade cookies.

WAIPIO WAYSIDE BED & BREAKFAST INN, P.O. Box 840, Honokaa, HI 96727; (800) 833-8849; (808) 775-0275; Jacqueline Horne, owner. Five rooms: two with private baths, two with shared bath, and one with half-bath. Rates: $50 to $80, single; $60 to $90, double, including full breakfast. Children welcome; no pets (two cats in residence); smoking allowed outside only; Visa/MasterCard. Waipio Valley, Kalopa State Park, and weekend theatre nearby. Jolene's Kay Kay korner in Honokaa and Mean Cuisine in Waimea recommended for dining.

DIRECTIONS: drive 2 miles past Honokaa on Hwy. 240 and look for a long white picket fence on the right. Turn into the second driveway for parking.

The rustic exterior and garden.

OUR PLACE PAPAIKOU'S B&B

Cathedral ceilings, lush gardens

The Hamakua Coast, north of Hilo, may be thriving with lush tropical vegetation, but you needn't go further than the back door of Our Place to experience it. This unusually-shaped home is perched like the weathered prow of a ship above a rushing stream and dense jungle. The stream can be heard but hardly seen because of the thick foliage.

The guest quarters of this cedar home are on the second level. (The hosts live on the bottom floor.) Here you will find that the "ship's prow" is actually a great gathering room, highlighted by cathedral ceilings, long couches, a fireplace, and grand piano. Glass doors slide open to a narrow, screened lanai that runs the entire length of the house. Several of the bedrooms, which appear somewhat dark because of their wood panelling, also have private access doors to the lanai.

Left, the towering spaciousness of the living room.

Hosts Sharon Miller and her sister, Ouida Trahan welcome their guests with relaxed Southern drawls, a down-home sense of humor, and positively infectious laughs. Sharon says their accent is such an oddity in the little town of Papaikou that "people here ask us what country we're from." Ouida, a retired M.D., is the green thumb behind the lush gardens here. In addition to cultivating a wide variety of tropical flowers, she is learning how to grow medicinal plants for use in her study of Chinese medicine. Guests leave with their yin and yang well balanced from Ouida's super-healthy breakfasts of organic tropical fruit, homemade granola, and banana nut bread.

Situated only four miles north of Hilo, Our Place provides a convenient, casual base for exploring the east side of the Big Island.

OUR PLACE PAPAIKOU'S B&B, 8 Mamalohoa Highway, P.O. Box 469, Papaikou, HI 96781; (800) 245-5250; (808) 964-5250; Sharon Miller and Ouida Trahan, owners. Four rooms, three with shared baths. Rates: $50 to $65, including continental plus breakfast. Two-night minimum. Children over 12 welcome; no pets (one German shepherd in residence); no smoking indoors; no credit cards. Hawaii Tropical Botanical Gardens, Akaka Falls, Lyman House Museum and Mission House nearby. Lehua's Bay City Bar & Grill, Restaurant Fuji, and Pescatore recommended for dining.

DIRECTIONS: from Hwy. 19, 4 miles north of Hilo, turn left at Pinky's Store. Turn left at first intersection and left again at the fifth driveway.

WAIMEA GARDENS COTTAGE

One of the Island's premier B&Bs

Considering that Barbara Campbell books only the very best bed and breakfasts through her statewide reservation service, it's no surprise that her own cottage is one of the top B&B's on the islands. Having traveled the world and personally inspected almost every B&B in Hawaii, Barbara knows *exactly* what her guests are looking for.

Set in the heart of the Parker Ranch cattle country, Waimea Gardens Cottage is actually one long cottage divided into two lovingly decorated units, each with its own private entrance. (The hosts live in another house across the garden.) The wood-shingled exterior is trimmed in blue-green, with colorful window boxes, multi-paned windows, and French doors opening to flowery brick patios. The adjacent stream and rolling green foothills of the Kohala Mountains form a pastoral backdrop to the cottage.

The first cottage, or Kohala Wing, features a rustic, century-old entry and quaint, country décor reminiscent of Hansel and Gretel. Copper pans hang in the kitchen while paintings by local artist Pegge Hopper hang on the walls. The newer Waimea Wing is decorated in a more sophisticated country charm. Sunlight streams through the lace curtains onto a crisp, striped loveseat with linen pillows. A koa rocker sits before the fireplace on polished wood floors. Soft pink walls are accented by dark green paint and wainscoting. An archway frames a bed which is covered with crisp floral linens. The bathroom is all white, light and spotless.

The hosts have thought of your every need, down to a sewing kit and iron. Among the many extras are welcome chocolates, flannel *yukata* robes, piles

Left, above, the Waimea Wing exterior. Below, Waimea Wing guest room.

Barbara and Charlie Campbell.

of Ralph Lauren towels, a sizeable dressing area, an armoire fitted with television and games, fresh flowers, and the morning paper delivered to your door.

WAIMEA GARDENS COTTAGE, Waimea (Kamuela); Barbara and Charlie Campbell, hosts; (800) 262-9912; (808) 885-4550; two one-bedroom cottages, one with full kitchen, one with kitchenette; both with private bath and patio. Rates: $110 to $115, including provisions for a generous self-serve breakfast (3 night minimum). Children welcome; no pets (two outdoor cats on premises); smoking limited to outdoors; no credit cards. Hapuna Beach, Waipio Valley, Pololu Valley, and Waimea's Kahilu Theatre nearby. Horseback riding available in Waimea and Kohala Mountains. Merriman's (one of the best restaurants on the Big Island), Eidelweiss, and Mean Cuisine recommended for dining.

DIRECTIONS: sent prior to departure.

Kohala Mountains from the cottage's yard.

Waimea Wing sitting room.

The entry way, made of Koa wood posts.

Cathedral-ceilinged guest room looks out on the ocean.

MAKAI HALE

A rhapsody in blue

Makai Hale has a commanding location in an exclusive, gated community high above the Kohala Coast. The expansive vista from this contemporary private home is a striking study in shades of blue: the light blue sky, the deep blue ocean, and the azure blue of the swimming pool.

The zen-like view is enhanced by the clean design of the home and its adjacent guest wing. Set on opposite sides of the pool, the two buildings are joined by a covered walkway lined with pillars made from gnarled ohia trees. (One of Hawaii's hardest trees, ohias develop their gnarled look from the vines that grow tightly around them.) Instead of the usual tropical landscaping, the house is surrounded by a stark rock garden and little pagodas.

The guest wing is sunny and immaculate, decorated in cheerful florals and white summer furniture. The main bedroom has a cathedral ceiling and full ocean view. From here you can step out the door directly to a small Jacuzzi.

Left, the striking pool overlooking the ocean.

Hosts Jerry and Audrey, a working couple, both grew up on the islands. They welcome their guests with an imaginative basket of locally-produced goodies such as macadamia nuts, taro chips, shrimp chips, and Kona coffee candies. While lounging by the pool, Audrey might even bring you afternoon *pupus*, or appetizers.

Makai Hale is only ten minutes north of the big resorts and superb beaches of the Kohala Coast. Close by are Hapuna Beach and Lapahaki State Park, two of the best white sand beaches on the Big Island. This area around Kawaihae is known for its sunny skies, and from December to May the whale watching is fabulous.

MAKAI HALE, Kohala Coast, Hawaii; *represented by Hawaii's Best Bed & Breakfasts;* (800) 262-9912; (808) 885-4550; One guest suite accommodates a party of up to four persons. Rates: $90 single, $95 double, including self-serve continental breakfast (2-night minimum). Children over 12 welcome; no pets; no smoking; Japanese spoken; no credit cards. Four miles to the island's best beaches. Polulu Valley, snorkeling at Lapakahi State Park, and golfing nearby. Cafe Pesto recommended for dining nearby; easy drive to Kohala coast luxury resorts or Waimea restaurants.

DIRECTIONS: sent prior to departure.

Two lanais with ocean views.

Rose Singarella and her lovebird, Mango.

KAILUA PLANTATION HOUSE

A romance with the ocean

Talk about being right on the ocean! The Kailua Plantation House is so close to the pounding surf that you can feel its fine mist from the lanai. If you love hearing the sound of the waves from your bed, this is the place to be.

A romantic, oceanfront setting is only one of this inn's many memorable highlights. Built in a crisp, new plantation style, the pink-and-white, two-story mansion has a fresh, bright look throughout, aided by lots of windows and skylights. As you are welcomed into the sunny living room, the sound of soft New Age music and sight of the surf just outside will immediately lower your blood pressure. The lanai overlooks an angular dipping pool that juts out over the black lava rocks in what Rose, the innkeeper, calls a "boomerang shape." The pool is crowned by a Jacuzzi and tiki torches that are lit at night.

The décor of the guest rooms ranges from tropical to Victorian to African. They feature all the comforts of a mainland-style inn—phones, refrigerators, televisions, and plush, private bathrooms. The platform baths in the Kai O Lani ("Heavenly Waters") and

Left, above, the Pilialoha Room. Below, the Hale Apelika Room.

Pilialoha ("Friendship") Rooms are pure bliss. Several bedrooms face the ocean, with prime views from their lanais. One could sit here all afternoon just watching cruise ships, outrigger canoes, people parasailing, and migrating whales gliding through Kailua Bay. The glass-enclosed shower of Kai O Lani even has an ocean view, so you never have to take your eyes from the sea.

In only a few years the Kailua Plantation House has earned a top-notch reputation, due in no small part to the warmth and pampering of resident innkeeper Rose Singarella. Her sidekick, a sweet little lovebird named Mango, is always perched affectionately on Rose's shoulder.

KAILUA PLANTATION HOUSE, 75-5948 Alii Drive, Kailua-Kona, HI 96740; (808) 329-3727; Rosanna Singarella, manager. Five rooms, all with private baths. Rates: $120 to $185, including full buffet breakfast with a different entrée every day. Weddings and receptions can be arranged. No children under 12; no pets; smoking allowed outside only; Visa/MasterCard/American Express. All water sports (including submarine rides), tennis and golf nearby. Palm Cafe and Canoe house recommended for dining.

DIRECTIONS: from the Keahole (Kona) Airport, follow Hwy. 19 south for 7 miles to Kailua-Kona. Turn right on Palani Rd., which turns into Alii Dr. Proceed through downtown and continue for about 1 mile to the inn, on the right.

Bathroom of the Kai O Lani Room, with its platform tub.
Overleaf, the unbelievably dramatic contrast made by the dipping pool set on the volcanic rock.

An oceanfront guest room.

A beachfront hammock.

Architectural gem on the beach

Hale Malia ("House of Marie") is another wonderful oceanfront bed and breakfast just two miles south of Kailua-Kona. Like the Kailua Plantation House, this home is dramatically close to the crashing waves. Hale Malia has the added feature of a narrow beach down by the lava rock shore. From here, a hammock sways temptingly under the coconut palms.

Named after its cheerful hostess, Marie, this private home is newly built in the old plantation style, with Victorian trim and antique furnishings. The charming millwork and array of droll cow themes found here and there lend a whimsical air to the house.

You first enter a vast, light-filled living room with high cathedral ceilings that never seem to end. The white walls and creamy carpet are accented by blue floral furnishings. A whole wall of windows provide an unhindered view of the ocean. Outside is a long, plantation-style lanai with white wicker chairs. One of the two bedrooms faces the ocean, its sliding glass doors opening directly onto the lanai.

Marie is a multi-talented woman with a great sense of humor. A helicopter pilot in her former life, she also designed most of her own home.

Left, newly built in the old plantation style.

HALE MALIA, Kailua-Kona, Hawaii; *represented by Hawaii's Best Bed & Breakfasts;* (800) 262-9912; (808) 885-4550. Two rooms, each with private bath. Rates: $95 to $115, including full breakfast (2-night minimum). No children; no pets; no smoking; no credit cards. Kahaluu Beach, Hulihee Palace, boating, shopping, coffee farms, and deep-sea fishing nearby. Palm Cafe and Huggo's recom-.nended for dining.

DIRECTIONS: sent prior to departure.

All the pretty patchwork quilts and pillows found throughout the house are Marie's creations, too. Having a house this close to the ocean requires the maintenance of a ship, and she keeps it in absolute tip-top shape. Marie also provides plenty of thoughtful extras—hair dryers in the bathrooms, a television in each bedroom, a washer and dryer for guest use, and a full breakfast which might feature such delicacies as Marie's special macadamia nut pancakes with passion fruit syrup.

While breakfasting on the lanai, guests can observe a colorful parade of boats and sea life. Pointing to the scene, Marie says, "I call this a slice of Hawaiiana."

The impressive two-story living room.

Overleaf, sitting on the beachfront lanai, the roar of the surf is music to one's ears.

ADRIENNE'S AT CASA DEL SOL B&B INN

Spanish-style elegance

Adrienne's at Casa Del Sol is newly-opened as a bed and breakfast, but as a private home it was already well-known for its prominent Mediterranean architecture—a stand-out in Kailua-Kona. Its red tiled roof, archways, and black, Spanish-style grillwork contrast strikingly with the usual plantation architecture found throughout Hawaii.

Hosts Adrienne and Reginald Batty are no newcomers to innkeeping, having previously operated another bed and breakfast down the coast. As this B&B is considerably more upscale than the other Adrienne's, they are justifiably excited about their elegant new digs.

The large, multi-level home sits across the street from Lyman's Point beach, a rocky spot where bigtime surfing championships are held. From the tiled poolside terrace and bedroom lanais, guests have a bird's-eye view of the busy surfer scene. Among the other gathering areas are a formal living room with piano (that guests are invited to use), a family room with big-screen television and VCR (supplemented by Adrienne's unbelievably large video library), and another lanai with a barbecue area. Breakfast, presided over by Reginald, is served in the dining room or on the poolside lanai. Bedrooms are scattered throughout the house, most facing the ocean with their own lanais. Some units are more like apartments, with their own separate entrances and kitchens.

Downtown Kailua-Kona is full of tourist action just two miles down Alii Drive. After a day of

The courtyard and pool show off the Spanish architecture.

sightseeing and swimming, guests can return for a soak in the spa and witness what Adrienne describes as "killer sunsets."

ADRIENNE'S AT CASA DEL SOL B&B INN, 77-6335 Alii Drive, Kailua-Kona, HI 96740; (800) 395-2272; (808) 326-2272; Adrienne and Reginald Batty, hosts. Five rooms, three with private baths and two with shared bath. Rates: $80 to $195, single; $80 to $250, double; $15 for each additional person; includes full breakfast. Children 16 and over welcome; no pets; smoking allowed on poolside lanai only; Visa/MasterCard. Swimming, snorkeling, kayaking, golfing, tennis, bicycling, and Kailua-Kona sights nearby. Jameson's By the Sea and Kona Inn Restaurant recommended for dining.

DIRECTIONS: from Keahole (Kona) Airport, follow Hwy. 19 south to Kailua-Kona. Turn right on Palani Rd. and proceed through downtown. When Palani Rd. turns into Alii Dr., continue $3\frac{1}{4}$ miles until you see a lava rock sign on the left that says "Casa Del Sol."

Left, above, the front of the casa, with its sign mounted on a wall made of volcanic rock. Below, view of Lyman's Point beach from the casa.

The elegant living room displays unusual antiques.

Hosts Adrienne and Reginald Batty.

DURKEE'S COFFEELAND BED & BREAKFAST

Fresh coffee and twinkling stars

Ever wonder exactly where Kona coffee comes from? Head south of Kailua-Kona and you'll soon find out. These coastal foothills in upcountry Kona are the very source of the rich, dark brew, and here is your chance to stay on a working coffee farm and see how it's all done.

Situated on two tropical acres, Durkee's is a small-scale farm of about four hundred coffee trees. Each year, from July to February, you literally wake up and smell the coffee beans in the air. Owners Marilyn and Chuck Durkee pick an annual average of eight thousand pounds of beans and process them right on the grounds. Guests can watch all of this—the picking, pulping, and drying—and enjoy the benefits of home-grown Kona coffee with their breakfast. The Durkees also grow a variety of tropical fruits that they pick fresh for breakfast.

Left, above, varieties of palms decorate the front yard. Below, owner Chuck Durkee drying coffee beans.

Famous Hawaiian Kona coffee beans.

Hot tub on the lanai.

The house itself is casual and unassuming, with simple accommodations either in the main house or in a private downstairs apartment. A large inviting deck overlooks the distant ocean, and from the hot tub, hammock or telescope, you can enjoy a knock-out view. The stars are often incredible up here. Says Marilyn: "Even guests from Alaska say they've never seen stars this clear."

While Marilyn runs the B&B with a warm and welcoming hand, Chuck is the green thumb of the grounds. In addition to the coffee and fruit trees (every one of which he planted from seed), Chuck cultivates over one hundred varieties of orchids in the front garden.

Guests like the fact that Durkee's is such a comfortable, laid-back place to stay. It has a quiet, country setting, yet is only minutes from the tourist action of Kailua.

DURKEE'S COFFEELAND BED & BREAKFAST, P.O. Box 596, Holualoa, Hawaii, HI 96725; (808) 322-9142; Marilyn Durkee, innkeeper. One room in main house and one garden apartment, both with private baths. Rates: $60, single; $75, double, including breakfast. Children not encouraged; no pets (dogs and cats on premises); smoking allowed on lanai only; no credit cards. Snorkeling, swimming, hiking, horseback riding, golf, and shopping nearby. The hosts are great sport-fishing enthusiasts. Several good restaurants in area.

DIRECTIONS: seven miles south of Kailua-Kona in the Keauhou-Kona area. Less than a half-mile off the Old Mamaloha Highway. Map and directions included in welcome letter.

HOLUALOA INN

A showcase of beautiful woods

This serene jewel is set on a quiet mountainside high above Kailua Bay in the artist's village of Holualoa. Surrounded by twenty acres of pasturelands, the Holualoa Inn is part of the Twigg-Smith Estate, which also encompasses a working coffee farm and cattle ranch. Desmond Twigg-Smith, nephew of the original owner, runs the inn with his staff while various members of his family are involved with the other domains.

The all-cedar, three-level home is an exquisite showcase of wood topped by distinctive copper roofing. Koa rockers and teak furnishings are gracefully poised on luxurious expanses of polished eucalyptus floors. Each common room opens easily to the next until, almost without realizing it, you find yourself out of doors. Fine artwork—painted by Desmond's mother and father—add bold splashes of color to the warm wood paneling of the dining room, billiards room, and various common areas.

Four guest rooms—each decorated in an elegantly understated tropical style—are distributed among the three levels, affording maximum privacy. From

The pool, with Kona Bay in the distance (see also pages 84–85).

every level there are sweeping views of the distant sea. Two gazebos—one by the swimming pool and another on the rooftop—provide ornamental lookouts. A luxurious tiled pool, its bottom painted with a red torch ginger blossom, also overlooks the panorama. At this lofty elevation, you feel utterly removed from all worldly weights. The serenity is indeed, as many guests have commented, "a little bit of heaven on earth."

Guests are welcome to take a tour of the family's forty-acre coffee plantation and see how coffee is grown, milled and roasted. They can enjoy home-grown Holualoa Kona coffee with breakfast and even buy a bag to take home with them.

Left, the Billiard Room, a popular gathering place for the guests.

The beautiful wood floor of the lanai.

HOLUALOA INN, P.O. Box 222, Holualoa, HI 96725; (800) 392-1812; (808) 324-1121; Desmond Twigg-Smith, owner. Four rooms, all with private baths. Rates: $125 to $175, including continental breakfast. No children; no pets; smoking permitted outdoors only; Visa/MasterCard/American Express. Weddings can be arranged at the inn. Gallery hopping and art classes offered in Holualoa Village. Kona is 15 minutes away. The Chart House and Palm Café recommended for dining.

DIRECTIONS: from Keahole (Kona) Airport, follow Hwy. 11 south past Kailua-Kona to Hualalai Rd. and turn left. Climb into the hills and turn left on Hwy. 180 to Holualoa Village. The inn's entrance is in the center of the village on the makai (ocean) side of the highway between Paul's Place general store and the Country Frame Shop.

The Garden Room.

The manicured lawn and garden of fruit trees.

MERRYMAN'S B&B

Country breakfasts in the tropical foothills

Just two miles from Merryman's you can snorkel and swim with the dolphins at Kealakekua Bay. Or, if you prefer, rent a kayak for two and paddle across the bay to the Captain Cook Monument. These are just a few of the helpful hints that Don and Penny Merryman will offer when you stay with them. They like to make sure that their guests don't waste any time trying to find their way around. Not only have they written out a personal beach guide, but they'll even provide you with the snorkeling equipment.

The Merrymans have a cheery modern home in the tropical foothills of Kealakekua, about fifteen minutes south of Kailua-Kona. Penny, a former florist, has a great eye for color and has decorated the whole B&B like a sunny country cottage. Against a background of white walls and wicker are pretty florals, bright bouquets of fresh flowers, and a collection of old-fashioned English plates. Guests can choose from among four rooms, all equally pretty, either with an ocean or garden view.

Left, above, the wicker-filled lanai. Below, the Rose Suite, one of four guest rooms with ocean or garden views.

At the entry to the common living room is a basket of cozy flannel slippers for guests to change into. The white-wicker-filled lanai overlooks a manicured lawn and garden of tropical fruit trees.

In the morning, everyone gathers for a breakfast of fresh fruit, Kona coffee, juice, and the chef's daily special, which might be eggs Florentine, Don's famous quiche, or sweet bread French toast.

This beautiful mountainous coast of the Big Island is quaint and rural, a land of tiny communities, small coffee farms, and cattle ranches. Aside from snorkeling and kayaking in Kealakekua Bay, you can also visit the nearby Place of Refuge, a sacred Hawaiian *heiau* set dramatically on the ocean.

MERRYMAN'S BED & BREAKFAST, P.O. Box 474, Kealakekua, Hawaii, HI 96750; (808) 323-2276; Don and Penny Merryman, owners. Four rooms, two with private baths and two with shared bath. Rates: $65 to $85, single; $75 to $95, double, including hearty Hawaiian breakfast. Well behaved children welcome; no pets; smoking allowed outside only; Visa/MasterCard/Discovery. All water sports, hiking, biking and horseback riding nearby. Aloha Cafe and Teshima's recommended for dining.

DIRECTIONS: sent with confirmation.

KALAHIKI COTTAGE

An all-day guided eco-tour

Kalahiki Cottage may be set on a working cattle ranch but it's far from provincial. In fact, this may be one of the most luxurious introductions to the Big Island that you could possibly experience.

The graceful, one-story cottage sits across the swimming pool from the main family house, which belongs to your hosts, Ray and Cynnie. Outside is a large lanai, attractively furnished with rockers, leather couches, a television, stereo, VCR, and even a kitchen and bar. Inside, the elegant, high-ceilinged bedroom features an antique koa dresser and carved bed that is covered with a creamy, embroidered feather comforter. There is also a separate dressing area and a spotless, all-white, state-of-the-art bathroom with its own private lanai facing the tropically-landscaped hillside.

As the third generation to run this sophisticated ranch (Cynnie's grandfather started it at the turn of the century), Hawaiian-style hospitality comes easily to the hosts. They provide their guests with everything from a welcome decanter of sherry to afternoon snacks to breakfast provisions. Little arrangements of fragrant flowers are placed throughout the cottage, as are plush terry robes for the pool and Jacuzzi. Guests are also invited to use the living room and lanai of their main house, which is gorgeously furnished in koa.

The only rural thing about the cottage is its setting on fifteen thousand private acres. To the east, you can look across miles of unspoiled native Hawaiian forestland—one of the biggest intact forest areas on the Big Island. It is also sanctuary to several endangered species of Hawaiian birds, including the alala (Hawaiian crow). By prior arrangement, Ray and Cynnie can organize an all-day, guided eco-tour through the ranch. A four-wheel-drive jeep will take you to hidden places and wildlife that otherwise would be unreachable.

Left, a decorative antique Koa dresser and bed (shown reflected in the mirror).

KALAHIKI COTTAGE, Honaunau, Hawaii; *represented by Hawaii's Best Bed & Breakfasts;* (800) 262-9912; (808) 885-4550. A one-bedroom cottage with kitchen plus one room in main house; both with private baths. Rates: $95 to $125, including self-serve continental breakfast (2-night minimum). Ranch eco-tour available at additional cost. Children over 12 welcome; no pets (outside dog in residence); no smoking; no credit cards. City of Refuge, Hookena Beach, and Kealakekua Bay nearby. Half-hour drive to restaurants; suggest bringing barbecue provisions.

DIRECTIONS: sent prior to departure.

Afternoon cheese and crackers.

A deck and garden open off the bathroom.
Overleaf, the cottage fronts on the pool between it and the main house.

RESERVATION AGENCIES

HAWAII'S BEST BED & BREAKFASTS. Barbara and Susan Campbell. P.O. Box 563, Kamuela, HI 96743; (800) 262-9912; (808) 885-4550; Fax (808) 885-0550. Booking service which caters exclusively to Hawaii's finest, most carefully-selected lodgings.

VOLCANO RESERVATIONS. Lisha Crawford. P.O. Box 998, Volcano, HI 96785; (800) 736-7140; (808) 967-7244. Select statewide accommodations.

HAWAII ISLAND BED AND BREAKFAST ASSO-CIATION. P.O. Box 1890, Honokaa, HI 96727. Publishes a brochure listing 40–45 B&B's on the Big Island.

ANN & BOB BABSON'S RESERVATION SERV-ICE. Ann and Bob Babson. 3371 Keha Dr., Kihei, Maui, HI 96753; (800) 824-6409; (808) 874-1166; Fax (808) 879-7906. Statewide B&B's, cottages, condominiums, and car rentals.

ALL ISLANDS BED & BREAKFAST. Ann Carlin. 823 Kainui Dr., Kailua, HI 96734; (800) 542-0344; (808) 263-2342. Statewide private guest accommo-dations, car rentals and inter-island flights.

BED & BREAKFAST HAWAII. Evie and Ed Davis. P.O. Box 449, Kapaa, Kauai, HI 96746; (800) 733-1632; (808) 822-7771; Fax (808) 822-2723. Statewide homestays, cottages, apartments and suites.

MY ISLAND BED & BREAKFAST. P.O. Box 100, Volcano, HI 96785; (800) 736-7110; (808) 967-7216; Fax (808) 967-7719.

HAWAIIAN ISLANDS BED & BREAKFAST AND VACATION RENTALS. Rick Maxey. 1277 Moku-lua Dr., Kailua, Oahu, HI 96734; (800) 258-7895; (808) 261-7895; Fax (808) 262-2181. Statewide B&B's and vacation rentals.

Left, sunrise on Kailua Bay, Oahu, near Hale Makai. *Overleaf, moonrise on Kailua Bay, Oahu, near Hale Makai.*